JOHN WILLIAMSON NEVIN

*American
Theologian*

Recent Titles in the
RELIGION IN AMERICA SERIES
Harry S. Stout, General Editor

JOHN
WILLIAMSON
NEVIN ❧

American
Theologian

RICHARD E. WENTZ

New York • *Oxford* • *Oxford University Press* • *1997*

Oxford University Press

Oxford   New York
Athens   Auckland   Bangkok   Bogota   Bombay   Buenos Aires
Calcutta   Cape Town   Dar es Salaam   Delhi   Florence   Hong Kong
Istanbul   Karachi   Kuala Lumpur   Madras   Madrid   Melbourne
Mexico City   Nairobi   Paris   Singapore   Taipei   Tokyo   Toronto

and associated companies in
Berlin   Ibadan

Copyright © 1997 by Richard E. Wentz

Published by Oxford University Press, Inc.
198 Madison Avenue, New York, New York 10016

Oxford is a registered trademark of Oxford University Press

Library of Congress Cataloging-in-Publication Data
Wentz, Richard E.
John Williamson Nevin : American theologian / Richard E. Wentz.
    p.   cm.—(Religion in America series)
Includes bibliographical references and index.
ISBN 0-19-508243-5
1. Nevin, John Williamson, 1803–1886.   2. Theologians—United
States—Biography.   3. Reformed Church—United States—Doctrines—
History—19th century.   4. Mercersburg theology.   I. Title.
II. Series: Religion in America series (Oxford University Press)
BX9593.N4W46   1997
230'.57'092—dc20
[B]   96-12652

9 8 7 6 5 4 3 2 1

Printed in the United States of America
on acid-free paper

For Cynthia

PREFACE

At last I have been able to do what I have longed to do for many years. I have been permitted to share my understanding of an American thinker whose ideas do not often gain the attention of a major publisher. I am indebted to Cynthia Read, Executive Editor at Oxford University Press, for sharing my enthusiasm for the work of John Williamson Nevin and providing me with this opportunity. Generations of friends and acquaintances have influenced me in my work. Those who are familiar with the heritage of Mercersburg will no doubt know the name of Charles E. Schaeffer, longtime student of Mercersburg and a clergyman-administrator in the Evangelical and Reformed Church, who in his ninety-ninth year sent me his personal copy of Nevin's book *The Mystical Presence.* "Charlie" recognized in me an interest and a concern of which I was only dimly aware at the time. I have been encouraged by my friends John B. Frantz, professor of history at the Pennsylvania State University, and Robert W. Delp, professor of history emeritus at Elon College in North Carolina. John Payne, professor of church history at the Lancaster Theological Seminary, has shared his insights into the ideas of Nevin and Schaff. Of course, numerous scholars cited in the text have assisted me through their own careful scholarship. The archives of the Evangelical and Reformed Church Historical Society, located at Lancaster Theological Seminary, were available to me during summer research trips. Florence Bricker, director of the archives, was always very helpful. More recently, Kay Schellhase, new director of the archives, has been especially gracious. The University of Notre Dame permitted me to examine the correspondence and writing of Orestes Brownson, an experience I found enjoyable and profitable. Faculty grants-in-aid from Arizona State University have supported the costs of travel and hospitality for visits to Notre Dame and Lancaster.

I have been fortunate to have a valuable collection of Mercersburg materials in my own library. The collection began during my years of association with the Mercersburg Academy and Trinity Reformed Church, located "at the foot of the hill." I discovered a stash of books in the basement of the building that housed the academy's library. When I asked the headmaster, Charles Tippetts, about those books he said, "Give me a list of what you want." The result was the personal acquisition of a full set of the *Mercersburg Review* and numerous other materials. The books have been my constant companions in the arid tundra of Arizona.

My most faithful critic has been my wife, Cynthia, a scholar in her own right who persistently challenges my logic and my most cherished assumptions. I owe her a great debt. She has supported my work and honed my critical skills, which often fall victim to my passion for ideas and my devotion to language. Whatever is effective about this profile of John Williamson Nevin is very much the result of her special love, her encouragement, and her astute intellect. Through the years I have been fortunate enough to have the technical assistance of the Humanities Computing Center of the College of Liberal Arts and Sciences at my university. Jim Dybdahl, word processor *extraordinaire,* has given me friendship and effort way beyond the call of duty. He has taken my handwritten copy and transformed it into the form most pleasing to a publisher. To Jim I am forever grateful. I would like to thank Kevin Jaques, research assistant in the Department of Religious Studies at Arizona State University, for his careful work on the preparation of the index.

When all is said and done, however, I must take total responsibility for what follows. I do so as one who is devoted to the study of religion in America and convinced of the significance of John Nevin as a much-neglected thinker in that history.

Tempe, Ariz.   R. E. W.
September 1995

CONTENTS

JOHN WILLIAMSON NEVIN

American Theologian

Introduction

John Williamson Nevin was born on February 20, 1803, in the Cumberland Valley of Pennsylvania and spent his early life on his parents' farm in Franklin County. His mother was a sister of Hugh Williamson, a prominent figure during the War of Independence and one of the framers of the Constitution. "Being of what is called Scotch-Irish extraction," he writes, "I was by birth and blood also, a Presbyterian; and as my parents were both conscientious and exemplary professors of religion, I was, as a matter of course, carefully brought up in the nurture and admonition of the Lord, according to the Presbyterian faith as it then stood."[1]

The "nurture and admonition of the Lord" were guided by Nevin's family and the common school, as well as the ministry of the Presbyterian Church of Middle Spring. Nevin later looked with great favor upon the orderly process represented by what he called the catechetical system, which entailed the use of biblical questions, a work called the *Mother's Catechism,* and the *Shorter Catechism* of the Westminster Assembly. Even pastoral visitation was conducted as a systematic examination within the comprehensive framework of the catechism. Young John studied Latin and Greek under the tutelage of his father, and ofttimes did so while working in the barn and the fields.

He entered Union College in Schenectady, New York, in the fall of 1817 at the tender and impressionable age of fourteen but managed to graduate with honors in 1821. His experience at Union disrupted the churchly order of his religious life by submitting it to the postulates of an emergent revivalism that gave priority to born-again testimony. Nevin spent two years at home on the farm, trying to find solace for the anxieties that plagued him and healing for the dyspepsia that agitated his body. He could find no secure sense of vocation, even though many at home and in the neighborhood assumed he would enter the Christian ministry. Finally, in the fall of 1823, he enrolled at Princeton Theological Seminary, "putting an end to much that had been painfully indeterminate before."[2] He found the scholarly world of Princeton pleasant and peaceful, and was in no hurry to consider the life that lay before him after seminary. The institution was at the center of the intellectual life of the Reformed tradition, its faculty revered by the entire Church. Princeton even served at that time as a seminary for many outside the tradition, including Lutherans like Samuel S. Schmucker. This fact deserves careful consideration in relation to the process of Americanization that tended to homogenize American Protestantism.

John Nevin was spared the decision concerning his aptitude for pastoral ministry. At the beginning of his professional career at Princeton, Charles Hodge took the opportunity to study in Europe. For two years Hodge's position at Princeton would be filled by the recent graduate from Middle Spring Presbyterian Church. During this period Nevin wrote *Biblical Antiquities,* a book used widely under the auspices of the American Sunday School Union.

On October 2, 1828, Nevin was licensed as a minister by the Carlisle Presbytery, meeting in Philadelphia. For more than a year he preached and taught among the churches of his native region. However, prior to leaving Princeton he had already been selected to the chair of Biblical Literature in the new theological seminary being established by the General Assembly of the Church in Allegheny City, near Pittsburgh.

Nevin's work at Western Theological Seminary came to the attention of clergy and congregants of the German Reformed Church, who shared pastoral concern for the social and religious welfare of Pennsylvania and Maryland. He had been engaged in intensive study of German scholarship in church history and theology and was developing a critical perspective by means of which he came to question much of the American religious order. By 1840 he was prepared both in mind and spirit to respond to the call to join Friedrich Rauch on the faculties of Marshall College and the German Reformed theological seminary located in the village of Mercersburg, Pennsylvania, located not too far from his ancestral home.

Rauch's influence on Nevin was brief but profound. Rauch became ill and died on March 2, 1841, but not before he had impressed John Nevin with his philosophical and theological erudition, acquired as a native of Hesse-Darmstadt at the universities of Marburg, Giessen, and Heidelberg. Nevin's theology of the Church was increasingly at odds with the ideas and practices of American revivalistic Evangelicalism. He was to become a prophetic forerunner of those mid-twentieth-century American theologians who fashioned their thought in response to the German theological renaissance of their own time.

From 1840 to 1844 Nevin worked on several theological issues that led to the publication of his book opposing "new measures" revivalism, *The Anxious Bench*. At the same time he was studying the historical and theological foundations of the Reformed tradition, publishing some chapters on the Heidelberg Catechism that later were collected in *The Genius of the Heidelberg Catechism*. The contours of an Evangelical (read Protestant) Catholicism were taking shape in Nevin's thought.

Nevin's ideas gained support thanks to the appointment of Philip Schaff, who joined him in the faculty of the seminary in 1844. Schaff had just begun his theological career as a lecturer at the University of Berlin. His inaugural address, delivered on the occasion of his installation into the Mercersburg chair, proved to be quite controversial. *The Principle of Protestantism* appeared in book form in 1845 and included as part of its appendix Nevin's sermon on Catholic unity delivered at the Triennial Convention of the Dutch and German Reformed Churches at Harrisburg some two months before Schaff's inauguration. Schaff had quoted from this sermon in his address.

Thus began a collaboration that resulted in one of the most unique movements in American religious thought of the mid–nineteenth century. Nevin was its theologian and Schaff its historian, yet the works of both thinkers were solidly historical and earnestly theological. "In whatever light he may be viewed," wrote Frederick A. Gast in 1889, "Dr. Nevin occupies high rank among the distinguished men of his age. An eminent scholar, a profound theologian, an independent thinker . . . he exerted a powerful influence, which will not cease to be felt for many generations to come."[3] Perhaps Nevin's greatest work was *The Mystical Presence,* published in 1846. He was the editor of *The Mercersburg Review* from 1849 to 1853, where many of his essays on such subjects as liturgy, American sectarianism, early Christianity, Anglicanism, and the nature of Catholicism first appeared. In 1856 he evaluated the theology of his contemporary Horace Bushnell in an essay entitled "The Natural and the Supernatural."

Nevin was professor of theology at Mercersburg from 1840 to 1851. In 1841, with Rauch's death, he also became president of Marshall College in the same place, serving in that capacity until 1853. There followed a period (1853–61) of formal disengagement from the institutions of the Church. During much of this time Nevin sought to work through the implications of his strongly incarnational and catholic theology. Where in America was the Church that was most hospitable to the theological position he espoused? It was to be a time of considerable religious anxiety. For, as Sydney Ahlstrom has put it, the Mercersburg Theology of John Nevin "ran counter to too many ingrained American attitudes. . . . [It revealed] with startling clarity . . . the basically Puritan forms of church life which had become so pervasive in America."[4]

For Nevin there was to be no satisfactory resolution of the dilemma of American religious life. He could not become a Roman Catholic, in spite of the encouragement of people like Orestes Brownson and a keen interest expressed by members of the hierarchy of the Catholic Church. He could not become an Anglican because he found the Anglican agenda to be unhistorical in its notion of a pristine episcopacy before the days of Romanization. It was difficult for him to be at peace with the American religion that pervaded the Protestant churches. Perhaps it was only possible to remain loyal to the insights he had been given, to do what he could to further the cause of Evangelical Catholicism in the liturgy and life of the German Reformed Church, and to leave the rest to the God who, in Christ, promised to be with the Church to the end of time.

Nevin returned to Franklin and Marshall College, now located at Lancaster, to serve as professor of aesthetics and history from 1861 to 1866. He served the college as president from 1866 to 1876 and as professor of mental and moral philosophy from 1868 until 1876, when he retired to his home outside Lancaster, where he died on June 6, 1886.

The name of John Williamson Nevin has been part of my vocabulary for many years. Before I knew very much about what he had actually written, I held in my mind a kind of respect and veneration for what he represented as the primary theological exponent of what became known as the Mercersburg Theology or the Mercersburg Movement.

I am a native Pennsylvanian, raised in the tradition of the Reformed Church in the United States, a German denomination that united in 1934 with the Evangelical Synod of North America to form the Evangelical and Reformed Church. Since 1957 the latter denomination has become part of an extraordinary twentieth-century ecumenical merger called the United Church of Christ.

Churches of the German Reformed tradition are numerous in Pennsylvania, particularly east of the Cumberland Valley. Many generations of Pennsylvania Germans[5] have identified themselves as either "Reffemiert" or "Lutterisch" (Reformed or Lutheran); and the landscape of Penn's Woods has been sacralized by red-brick structures, featuring bell towers, and nurturing the lives of twin congregations—Lutheran and Reformed. In some ways the religious life of eastern Pennsylvania has been more Germanic than it has been confessionally Lutheran or Reformed. For the people of German heritage there has existed a precious ethnic religiousness that was at one time crucial to their existence as outsiders in a culture that was peremptorily English.[6] Their dialect and Germanic customs were aspects of their Americanization.

The middle decades of the nineteenth century were marked by considerable tension between the claims of past and present, history and immediacy, tradition and subjectivity, universality and particularity. There were the new revelations of Joseph Smith and Ralph Waldo Emerson and the renewal of confessionalism by theologians like the Lutheran Charles Porterfield Krauth. On the one hand, there was the experiential revivalism of Charles Grandison Finney and Phoebe Palmer, while, on the other, there was the renewed sacramentalism of John Henry Hobart. The American literary imagination struggled to find some means to understand the dullness, the lack of depth, in American life that seemed to accompany our feverish activity. These were times of adventure and of ennui. A grand inquiry into the fashion of the American soul was under way. How were we to become this new American Adam without losing the memory of the vision, the revelation, and the experience that were part of the past?

John Williamson Nevin was a contributor to the investigation of ultimate order and meaning that was taking place in the emergent new Republic of the early nineteenth century. He is a lesser-known thinker than Horace Bushnell or Nathaniel W. Taylor, lesser known than contemporaries like Orestes Brownson or Isaac Hecker. But he spoke mainly from the platform provided by his position as a professor in the little German Reformed college and theological seminary located in the remote Franklin County village of Mercersburg, Pennsylvania. Although by birth and early education a child of old school Presbyterians, and a graduate of Princeton Theological Seminary, Nevin had been called into service to an ethnic enclave of the Reformed tradition. It was in that context that he was encouraged to apply the insights of historical perspective and an incarnational theology to the circumstances of American religious life.

The denomination he chose to serve during most of his professional life had been torn by dissensions and diversity before John Nevin was called to provide leadership. The clergy of the German Reformed Church were at odds over issues of revivalism and other forces of Americanization that threatened to alter the classical Protestantism of Switzerland and the German Rhineland. The board of visitors of the seminary in Mercersburg encountered considerable difficulty in appointing a suitable professor to join Frederick Augustus Rauch when he remained the lone faculty member after the resignation of Lewis Mayer in 1839. However, there were those like the Reverend Samuel R. Fisher of Emmittsburg, Maryland, who had heard of John Nevin and his knowledge of German theology and literature and thought of him as the most promising candidate. Nevin was in some sense neutral to the internal politics of the Americanization process in the German Reformed Church, yet he understood the genius of the Reformed tradition and the German culture.

When Nevin accepted the call to serve the seminary in Mercersburg, he recognized an opportunity to deal with issues of catholicity, ethnicity, and denominationalism in a denomination that uniquely reflected these concerns in the evolving religious life of the American Republic. He knew the importance of the German Church in the history of the Reformation. "The spirit of a time-hallowed faith," he wrote, "is still enshrined in her articles and forms, and the German Church in this country has become a rising interest. No section of our American Zion is more important. None embraces vaster resources of power in proportion to its limits. None exhibits a richer intellectual ore, available in the same way for the purpose of religion."[7] From 1840 until his death in 1886, Nevin used the "resources of power" and the "intellectual ore" of the German Church to address the "American Zion."

Nevin's life and work are worthy of the careful attention of any scholar who wishes to address the formation of American religious thought in the nineteenth century. Perhaps he is not an intellectual virtuoso of the genius of a Kant or a Hegel, but he leads us into an understanding of American religion that is equal to the work of any nineteenth-century religious thinker.

What follows is not an intellectual biography in the modernist sense of that genre but rather a kind of postmodern portrait of Nevin's ideas. Yet I do not escape the modernist net entirely. After all, I have set forth the thesis that Nevin was very much an American theologian, and not merely a romantic misfit unable to find a home in the American intellectual landscape and without resource to become an expatriate. My attention to the public and dialectical character of Nevin's thought shapes the manner in which his work presents his life to us. In a certain sense I am in dialogue with Nevin. I address what I observe to be those themes that direct the course of Nevin's thought. They are themes that were crucial issues in the religious and cultural context of nineteenth-century America. Of course, I identify these themes from the perspective of a twentieth-century student of religion in America who is devoted to contextual understanding.

one

THE LIKENESS PRESERVED:
THE LIFE AND WORK OF
JOHN WILLIAMSON NEVIN

In the delightful essay "Zacharius Ursinus," published in 1851, John Williamson Nevin wrote of Ursinus:

> To understand his history and character, we need not so much to be familiar with the events of his life outwardly taken, as to know the principles and facts which go to make up its constitution in an inward view; and, of this, we can have no more true or honorable representation, perhaps, than the likeness that is still preserved of him in [the Heidelberg] Catechism.[1]

The events of Nevin's life outwardly taken are, indeed, worthy of our familiarity, but they tend to be ordered by the principles and facts that make up the constitution of Nevin's inward and intellectual world. The likeness of this nineteenth-century American educator and thinker is preserved in the pages of the *Mercersburg Review* and the *Reformed Church Messenger*.[2] However, there is no more true or honorable representation than the likeness preserved in Nevin's book *The Mystical Presence: A Vindication of the Reformed or Calvinistic Doctrine of the Holy Eucharist*. As Brian Gerrish notes, "It is . . . the work for which Nevin is best known, and it deserves to be ranked among the classics of American theological literature."[3] Yet *The Mystical Presence* will be recognized by very few Americans as such a work. Of course, some scholars of American religion have heard of it because of its close attention to historical inquiry and to such topics as the Eucharist and the doctrine of the Church—hardly popular theological topics in the age of Charles G. Finney and Andrew Jackson's common man. Yet, for all the public indifference to the subject, "the great central theme . . . around which all religious and theological movements revolve, is the Church Question,"[4] wrote Philip Schaff in 1846. John Williamson Nevin contemplated that question throughout his life.

THE OUTSIDER

The Mystical Presence is a very humanistic document reflecting the author's struggle to comprehend the historical significance of the Incarnation of Jesus Christ. It is an American text, part of the public discourse of the second third of the nineteenth century. In the preface Nevin asked:

> Is it true that the modern Protestant Church in this country has, in large part at least, fallen away from the sacramental doctrine of the sixteenth century? All must at least allow, that there is some room for asking the question. . . . For in the nature of the case, such a falling away, if it exist at all, must be connected with a still more general removal from the original platform of the Church. The Eucharistic doctrine of the sixteenth century was interwoven with the whole church system of the time; to give it up, then, must involve in the end a renunciation . . . of this system itself in its radical, distinctive constitution.[5]

For John Nevin, a substantive altering of history had taken place in the Incarnation of Jesus Christ, the significance of which is advanced and constructively celebrated in the Eucharist. "We have no right," he said, "to set the inward in opposition to the outward, the spiritual in opposition to the corporeal, in religion [by which he meant Christianity as at once the 'individual and general' of what religion itself means]."[6]

Nevin's ideas seem quite radical in the American context; yet by their very radicality they are American religious thought, not the mere transplantation of German and English (Coleridge) romanticism into the American setting. They are a dissenting statement, a deposition by one who discovered that he did not "fit in." Nevin's thought is the stance of an "outsider" to the elusive mainstream of American religion. Yet, as R. Laurence Moore reminds us, "[O]utsiderhood is a characteristic way of inventing one's Americanness."[7] There is a dilemma, however: Nevin's own agenda is directed against the fragmentary character of religious pluralism of nineteenth-century America as it was represented in his essay "The Sect System." Nevertheless, we know that members of sects are typically thought of as outsiders. The dilemma itself is uniquely American: Where else has the religious impulse toward universal significance been faced with the necessity of building those social and cultural foundations in a political order that required civility among competing claims

in an atmosphere of liberty, without coercion? Perhaps in America sectarianism is the mark of the insider, not the outsider. Nevin's thought took the
American dilemma seriously and espoused an interesting theological resolution that, in retrospect, seemed to founder on the shoals of the very issue that
frequently rose to the surface of his writing: the relationship between the
inward and the outward. Glenn Hewitt says of him: "True religion involved
both an inward, living force and external forms. The outward forms receive
their power from the inward force."[8] However, a comprehensive reading of
Nevin's thought leads to the conclusion that outward and inward work together in dialectical tension.

AN AMERICAN VOICE

The outward form of Nevin's own life is intricately bound up with the inward
force of his ideas. When we examine his life and published works, we are
face-to-face with the "principles and facts" that seemed to be the premises of
his existence. Nevin was a public theologian, constantly involved in response
to crises and issues in American religion and culture. As such, he was more a
historical theologian than a systematic theologian in the usual sense of the
word. Withal, he was very much an American theologian. Failure to recognize
this has been the cause of some confusion in the thinking of previous interpreters of the person and his work. Although James Hastings Nichols had a
genuine appreciation for the work of Nevin, he was too eager to assign him
to the hustings of romanticism and idealism.[9] This assignment also permitted
Nichols to characterize the significance of Nevin's thought as being quite
limited to the mid–nineteenth century. There were, of course, those in the
denominational circles in which Nevin found himself after his move to Mercersburg who also saw his influence as tangential to the inevitable progress of
theological liberalism. Luther Binkley, whose revised dissertation was published as *The Mercersburg Theology* in 1953, closed his preface with the words:
"Though in the course of historical development, we have *passed beyond the
specific doctrines* of the Mercersburg theologians, it is my hope to recapture their
humble spirit, their faithful historical scholarship, and their devoted search for
truth."[10] In his concluding comments, Binkley reaffirmed his belief that "as a
body of conviction the Mercersburg Theology is dead. All theologies have
their day and cease to be."[11] Perhaps Binkley, of course, realized that he had
refashioned one of Nevin's own dicta when he based his opinion on a notion
of "historical development." However, in Nevin's view, historical development
does not mean that theologies necessarily "have their day and cease to be."

John B. Noss, Binkley's mentor and professor of philosophy at Franklin and Marshall College, shared the notion that "few of us can adopt [the Mercersburg] position as it stands."[12] In these comments we may note the historian's predilection for hasty bracketing of historical significance. Many historians have been rather heavy-handed with their agendas, leading generations of readers to conclude that certain ideas and practices are readily consigned to the archives, where their only significance lies in their usefulness to the scholar who tries to clarify "past" contexts. However, history is more than our reading of it; and ideas and practices may not be confined to the historicist graveyards to which they are assigned.

Of course, a modernist theological agenda also lies beneath the comments of Binkley and Noss. What if the thought of John Williamson Nevin is of more than historical interest? Is that possible? The Mercersburg Theology has received renewed attention, perhaps beginning with the formation of the Mercersburg Society in the mid-1980s and the earlier publication of B. A. Gerrish's *Tradition and the Modern World,* in which he gave significant attention to Nevin's thought. Between the appearance of Nichols's and Gerrish's books, Claude Welch and Sydney Ahlstrom evaluated Nevin's thinking in, respectively, *Protestant Thought in the Nineteenth Century. Vol. 1, 1799–1870* and *Theology in America.*[13] However, Ahlstrom had already introduced Nevin's ideas into the mainstream of the study of American religious thought with the publication of his essay "Theology in America: A Historical Survey" in *The Shaping of American Religion.*[14] It may very well be that "few of us can adopt the Mercersburg position as it stands." Here we are not concerned with adopting but with understanding. We can certainly begin to recognize the significance of Mercersburg's primary theologian, John Williamson Nevin, as a major figure in the history of ideas in America. We can examine his thought not only as an antiquarian deposit but as a unique and living contribution to Christian thought and to American self-understanding. Few of us ever adopt a position as it stands, but we can permit the position of John Nevin to stand as a creative legacy. After all, what we call the past is as relevant to our understanding as is the present. Both are metaphors used to tell the story of the human experience of persistent change, a story that is greater than the individual episodes we conceive and relegate to arbitrary categories of past and present.

This book seeks to explore the relationship of John Nevin's inner life to some of the outward circumstances of American public life. This is the kind of biographical study that can have a thesis, inasmuch as it insists on telling Nevin's story by discussing the likenesses of him that have been preserved in his writings. The thesis is that the life of John Williamson Nevin is shaped in response to the circumstances of American life and thought, that it represents an ever-expanding awareness that horizons are never settled boundaries, that the self is discerned as it is opened to symbols that transmit a reality ever greater than our ability to comprehend. In Nevin's life this is played out dialectically, as he responds inwardly to outward evidences. As we shall see later in this study, Nevin's thought is hinged on the notion that great public events are providential moments in which we are faced with the necessity of appropriate inner resolution and response. He thought the Church to be evidence of a reality present in history (a new creation)—a reality not *ordinarily* observable or affirmable but a reality that provides the resource for appropriate response to public crises. A method of thinking and living emerges out of this presupposition: one must use the evidence of tradition and sacrament to find the appropriate inner resources to respond to public circumstance. Tradition and sacrament provide us with eyes to see and ears to hear.

All life is public, not individualistic. One must always be inwardly sure of outward claims and events; and the inner significance of outward events must always be discerned. These principles shaped the life of John Nevin and established a dialectical pattern of outward assessment and inner investigation in the light of one's faith in the constitution of grace and truth that lives in the Church as a result of the Incarnation. The dialectical pattern of Nevin's thinking is the likeness in which we may observe his life.

HIS LIFE IN PUBLIC VIEW

By the time John Nevin entered Union College, he had already been nurtured in the catechetical system of classical Presbyterianism. "The Presbyterianism prevalent in the Cumberland Valley at the beginning of the . . . century," writes Nevin's biographer, Theodore Appel, "was based throughout on the idea of covenant family religion, of church membership by a holy act of God in baptism; and, following this as a direct reference to their coming to the Lord's table."[15] The system of salvation, at least in theory, was churchly, representing a process of lifelong nurturing, instruction, and examination. However, changes were already at work in American Protestantism, including the Presbyterian tradition, that were to alter this system. It is perhaps not too much to say that much of the Lutheran and Reformed heritage brought to American shores reflected many of the churchly assumptions of the Catholic tradition of Christianity well into the nineteenth century. The dominance of Puritanism, the emergence of revivalism beginning in the eighteenth century, the individualistic bent of the religion of the American enlightenment, and the voluntaryism of the new nation—all combined to effect a new form of Christianity that we may call revivalistic Evangelicalism. The churchly tradition of the catholic substance of Christianity, shared by the Reformed and Lutheran traditions, was all but lost in the process.

Union College at the time of Nevin's arrival in 1817 was an institution representing an alliance of Protestant denominations, all committed to seeing to the redemption of the new nation and guaranteeing its moral integrity. Most of these denominations had accepted the necessity of revivals as a means of maintaining the order of Christian civilization.[16] There were revivalists like Asahel Nettleton, Timothy Dwight, and Lyman Beecher, who opposed demonstrative or "enthusiastic" religion and championed the maintenance of the existing social order and the orderly practice of worship and meetings. They were the old school Presbyterians and Congregationalists. However, these denominations were to be affected by the "new measures" revivalism of Charles Grandison Finney, whose influence on American religion and culture was extraordinary. Finney's movement was antistructure and individualistic, in spite of its emphasis on social reform.[17] There was active disagreement among the revivalists themselves concerning "new measures," and the threat to the social order was alleged by the old school leadership. Nevertheless, the revivalists agreed on one thing at least: that a singular experience of "conversion" was essential to the individual and to the practice of Christianity.

Young John Nevin was "converted" during a series of meetings conducted by Asahel Nettleton. This experience must probably be registered as one of the first major instances in which he was faced with the erosion of the dialectic of the inward and the outward. Nevin later understood the unsettling nature of his conversion experience as a descent into introspection, a kind of agitation of the inner self that could become a lifelong preoccupation. His "conversion" experience abstracted the inner life from its ongoing sustenance in the nurturing life of the Church. It was assumed among the revivalists that Nevin's "conversion" provided in some sense an opportunity to associate with a church, as if his early baptism and Christian nurture had been of no real consequence.

According to revivalistic Evangelicalism, the religious life was the inner life and had little to do with such external circumstances as education and the sacramental life of the Church. Nevin did not completely understand his difficulties at the time, but he returned to the Cumberland Valley from college in 1821, his whole being "in an invalid state, I was dyspeptic in body and mind." He was nineteen years old when he graduated from Union and unsure of his spiritual well-being or the direction of his life. For two years he tried to regain his bodily health and some resolution of the anxiety occasioned by his earlier conversion and the religious life at Union, divorced as it was from the educational system.

On the one hand, the services of Middle Spring Church now seemed formalistic and meaningless; on the other, there was the sense that the churches of Carlisle Presbytery were changing in response to the new religion in the making. Revivalistic Evangelicalism was replacing the churchly tradition. The young man's confusion continued, but the life of his father's farm administered a certain healing. He plowed and harrowed the acres of limestone soil; he rode horseback through the hills and fields, and developed a botanical interest in the study of plants and flowers. He did some writing for the public press and attended meetings of a debating society in the borough of Shippensburg.

His external life and health improved somewhat, and Nevin began to contend more realistically with the inward call to further study. What was it he should study? He liked the classical substance of the educational heritage. However, it had always been assumed that he would study for the ministry. Although he himself seemed unable to entertain the idea of any other profession, he was troubled by the facade of pietistic sentiment that seemed to linger over the clergy, particularly under the influence of revivalism. It had already entered his mind that inwardness without attention to external manifestation was individualistic and incomplete. Princeton, citadel of the Reformed tradition in America, was the place to study theology. Yet

> Princeton divinity students, so far as they had appeared among us yet in Shippensburg or Middle Spring, had a certain air of conscious sanctimony about them, which seemed to be rebuking all the time the common worldliness of these old congregations . . . and gave the notion of a *Young Presbyterianism,* which was in a fair way to turn into old-fogeyism soon all their existing religious life.[18]

There was an ambivalence about the new religiousness that made young Nevin cautious.

Scholars have frequently labeled this cautiousness as conservative. Certainly that is so, if by the use of the term "conservative" we allude to the human desire to function with a memory, to conserve and make use of what humankind has learned over the centuries. Yet John Nevin was not a reactionary, opposed to change, a champion of "old-fogeyism." Something told him that, in order to encounter change properly and deal with its essential call for inward response to necessary development, it is necessary to understand the responses of the past. The past lives in the present. He knew that true liberality of spirit requires more than simple adoption of every plaything on the winds of time.

Nevin was at Princeton from 1823 to 1828, the first three years as a student. Samuel Miller and Archibald Alexander were the established stars of the Princeton faculty, recently joined by the young Charles Hodge. For John Nevin the seminary years were a time of refuge and contemplation. He was uncertain of the uses he would make of his theological education and concentrated his energies on biblical and language studies. Even though the formal studies registered an appreciation for the churchly tradition of the Reformers, the practical religious life of the seminary seemed dominated by the new religiosity of American pietistic revivalism. This tension had a great deal to do with directing the young graduate away from the pastorate and toward a more academic career.

As it turned out, Charles Hodge was scheduled to visit Europe in order to prepare himself more adequately for his position at Princeton. A two-year study visit had been arranged, and John Nevin was offered an appointment as temporary replacement. "My studies," he wrote, "went on more effectively than ever, being aided now by the work of teaching others."[19] By the time Hodge returned from Europe in 1828, Nevin had published a book, *Biblical Antiquities,* for use by the American Sunday School Union, and had been singled out to be the first occupant of the chair of biblical literature in the theological seminary that was soon to open at Allegheny, Pennsylvania. However, financial difficulties prevented Western Seminary from opening for more than a year; accordingly, John Nevin placed himself under care of the Carlisle Presbytery and in October of 1828 was licensed to preach after passing the necessary examinations.

While he awaited the opening of the seminary in 1830, Nevin preached and lectured in churches and schoolhouses of the Cumberland Valley, gaining confidence in his commitment to the pulpit and developing a style of extemporaneous speaking that he distinguished from the "Methodistical ranting" often associated with popular preaching. In his own understanding, Nevin was becoming an expositor of "the evangelical truths of Christianity" in a reasonable and practical manner. This was a period in which he was coming to terms with some of the external realities associated with the practical life of the Church outside the precincts of college and seminary. Just as he was ready to begin his work at Western Seminary, he was again forced into the necessity for internal resolution. His father, who had been both an intellectual and a spiritual guide for so much of the younger Nevin's life, suddenly took ill and died. He had not only to deal with his own desolation but also, as firstborn, to assume responsibility for the family his father had left behind. "Here then was a new phase . . . quite as important for its subsequent character as my

going soon after to the Western Theological Seminary. I was to be, hencefor-
ward, in some measure at least, a man of business as well as a man of letters
and books." [20]

Nevin spent ten years at the seminary in Pittsburgh. It was a time of
speaking in his "Puritanic Presbyterian tongue" [21] about issues of moral reform. As a professor in the Western extension of the Christian civilization of
the East, Nevin had to be concerned about the life of the churches and the
people in a rapidly changing nation. He edited a weekly journal, *The Friend*
(the title supposedly influenced by his reading of Samuel Taylor Coleridge),
in which he boldly defended the personal moral virtues associated with the
benevolent societies in their quest for social reform. Temperance (meaning
abstinence from use of alcoholic beverages), piety, and opposition to infidelity,
ladies' fairs, theatrical entertainment, and fashionable amusement all served as
the catalog of Nevin's agenda. At the height of his moral concern was the
issue of slavery. Nevin was an abolitionist, although he "condemned [William
Lloyd] Garrison . . . and others of the same stripe, as being irreligious in
their spirit no less than unpatriotic." [22] His antislavery stance earned him the
opprobrium as a disturber of the peace and caused a prominent physician to
brand him "the most dangerous man in Pittsburgh." [23] Hewitt says of him
that, as his interest in theology and historical development grew, Nevin was
"less interested in policing individual morality" and his interest in ethics
moved to a much "deeper level." [24] Nevin had always been a man of reconciliation, never of "party spirit"; and his antislavery stance, like President Lincoln's, was set to find "common ground in regard to the great evil of slavery."
Nevertheless, among some Americans, to call slavery a "great evil," to call for
abolition and reconciliation, were themselves the disturbance of a false peace.

At the same time that Nevin was doing his duty on behalf of a nervous
Protestantism, concerned with its stability in the face of relentless change, he
was also trying to resolve the significance of his intuitive affinity for the principle of Christianity that lay hidden in the worldliness of the classical, churchly
Christianity. His moralism bothered him because it was in service to some
false religious need to control self and society by means of subjective experience and achievement. He began to recognize, especially through his reading
of German scholarship, that what he called material and formal principles
must exist in creative tension and that the problem of the material must in
some sense be settled before the formal can be effectively used. He claimed
that all literature, science, and art have a soul (material principle) that

> must be apprehended everywhere by inward soul-intuition . . . in order that
> the forms [formal principle] in which they come before us may ever have all
> their true sense and worth. But if this be so where merely natural life or

existence is in question, how much more must it hold good in the case of such absolutely supernatural truth as is confessed to form the inward matter and substance of the Holy Scriptures [formal principle]?[25]

So it was with Nevin's own life. "My existence . . . was not inwardly in full harmony with itself." A reigning American orthodoxy, as he put it, seemed satisfied that the Scriptures themselves were available to all, naturally considered—a supernatural truth contained in sacred text spoke directly to natural minds. What was missing in Nevin's life was something other than subjective experience or Scriptures themselves—some objective reality to which one could relate. "It is only the Divine itself in all revelation that can make it to be what the spirit seeks after in this form. . . . It is not by the outward that we see the inward; only by the inward can we understand the outward."[26]

But the inward for Nevin did not mean subjectivity. What he calls "spiritual intelligence" is the mode of existence that requires our use of "faith." Faith is the outward facing of the inward to that which is more than our own knowledge, yet directs that knowledge. Faith is response to the "supernatural object, which in its ultimate fullness is the Word Incarnate."[27] Only if the "eye of our spiritual intelligence" is directed by relationship to that Word (material principle) shall we be able to comprehend the meaning of it in Scripture (formal principle).

There is, of course, an aristocratic principle at work here. Certainly Nevin was reacting against the kind of democratization taking place in America and represented by the revivalism of the times.[28] It was, after all, the period in which "[t]he principle of orderly, regulated development gave way to a 'natural,' unsystematic, uncontrolled unleashing of the nation's energies. Jackson symbolized this freedom from control. The face of the country was changing, and in a way which caused apprehensions."[29] For Nevin it was all too "natural," unsystematic, and uncontrolled. He was discovering the meaning and significance of history. And he knew that the truth of certain forms of discourse is only available to those who are of a mind to receive it. That's why children are baptized. They are brought into the mind of the Body of Christ in order that their lives may be spent learning to understand the world with that mind. Ultimate truth is not so "naturally" and immediately accessible as Jackson's common and democratized humanity would have it.

Nevin had begun to learn the German language and to read the works of German thinkers like Isaac Dorner and August Neander. Neander in particular was to be a major force in providing the historical perspective that assisted Nevin in finding hermeneutical clarification for the affinity he had long felt for an incarnational theology that resisted the subjectivity of revival-istic Evangelicalism. In 1837, when Luther Halsey withdrew from the Western faculty, Nevin was asked to teach church history. The way was opened up for a greater disciplinary attention to both German and the study of history. The discovery of historical awareness was in itself a very religious awakening. "As I had studied it at Princeton," wrote Nevin, "it was for me the poorest of sacred science."[30] Dull, unscientific, and hardly sacred, it was not a particularly edifying course of study. Then, under Neander's guidance, the dead past suddenly appeared before him as a living present.

It was at this time of his life that John Nevin received an invitation to be professor of theology in the seminary of the German Reformed Church at Mercersburg, Pennsylvania. It must be remembered that there was considerable communication among the various ethnic branches of the Reformed tradition—Scotch-Irish Presbyterians, German and Dutch Reformed. Nevertheless, the invitation from a German-speaking tradition came somewhat as a surprise, and Nevin at first declined to be considered because he was not a native of the church and thought it would be difficult to be acceptable in the German ethos.

When Nevin came to Mercersburg in 1840, "the German Reformed Church was derelict but not dead."[31] It needed leadership and imagination to bring it to maturity in the American setting. Nevin had sole charge of the seminary until 1844, his colleague Frederick Rauch having died about ten months after Nevin's arrival. He gave himself unsparingly to the work of theology and to the presidency of Marshall College, the collegiate institution of the Church located on the same campus. Meanwhile, he was still struggling to find an appropriate method to clarify his understanding of Christianity and its relationship to human history. In his eulogy for Rauch, offered at the funeral ceremony on the occasion of the removal of Rauch's remains from Mercersburg to Lancaster on March 8, 1858, Nevin held: "Faith must embrace, not the notion of supernatural things simply, but the very power and presence of things themselves. The invisible was felt to be truly actual and real, while the outward and visible might be regarded as being in some sort only its empty shadow, projected in the field of space."[32] By the time Nevin penned these words he had run the course of almost two decades in the development of what became known as the Mercersburg theology, which bears the spirit of Rauch's German philosophy, Philip Schaff's principles of historical development, and Nevin's incarnational theology. Rauch, from the universities of Giessen and Heidelberg, had been heavily influenced by Hegelian philosophy and was one of the first to introduce those ideas into the American setting, especially with the publication of his book *Psychology*. He thought highly of

Nevin, but their anticipated collaboration was short-lived due to Rauch's un-expected death in March 1841.

Nevin struggled with the care of college and seminary until the arrival of Schaff late in 1844. Philip Schaff was Swiss, educated in Germany among some of the most renowned of nineteenth-century thinkers, including Friedrich Tholuck, Ferdinand Christian Baur, Isaac Dorner, Julius Müller, and August Neander. Schaff was to be as important to the maturation of Nevin's thought as Rauch had promised to be. He had lived in the very environment that produced the ideas so relevant to Nevin's own search for a hermeneutic to perfect his own thinking. The problem of the dialectic of the inward and outward needed the support of creative philosophy and the new sense of his-tory. Schaff professed to have received the concept of development from Baur and expounded it in his inaugural lectures, *The Principle of Protestantism,* and in a subsequent work, *What Is Church History?* Latent in the notion of historical development was a metaphysical insight that would prove useful to Nevin's theology, dedicated as he was to the incarnational value of the continuing presence of the Church in the world.

John Williamson Nevin remained at Mercersburg until 1852, when he resigned his positions in order to deal with the crises of his life. He had spent a full decade expending his energies as a scholar, teacher, writer, and administrator in what must have been very stressful circumstances. His think-ing had addressed the public dimensions of the emergent culture of the nation in the antebellum period. He had struggled to give some intellectual stability to the German Reformed Church during its efforts to come of age in the American setting. And he had discovered aspects of the nature of Christianity that made him increasingly uncomfortable with the spirit of Protestantism as it was developing in this country. He needed rest and time for contemplation; he needed to gain perspective and distance from the circumstances of his frus-tration.

THE LIFE IN THE WORKS

During the Mercersburg decade Nevin published an amazing amount of highly controversial material. *The Anxious Bench* (1843–44) was a critique of new measures revivalism, perhaps one of the best of such documents produced in the nineteenth century. The ideas set forth in this book invite the attention of anyone who wants to understand what was happening to American society at the time. In it Nevin writes:

A whole Babel of extravagance has been let loose upon the community far and wide in the name of religion. . . . A revival is one thing, and a Phrygian dance another; even though the Phrygian dance should be baptized into Christian montanism. Life implies action, but all action is not life. . . . The ground of the sinner's salvation is made to lie at last in his own separate person. . . . All stress is laid upon the energy of the individual will (the self-will of the flesh) for the accomplishment of the great change in which regeneration is supposed to consist.[33]

The reader will note the manner in which the style and content of Nevin's thought ran against the swelling stream of individualism and antiintellectualism that had begun to characterize American life. The constructive side of *The Anxious Bench* was a statement on behalf of a "system of Catechism." It was not a fully developed conception and probably appears to the reader to be somewhat reactionary. However, the system of which he writes is a holistic way of regarding the truth present in the Christian dispensation. The system of the catechism assumes a tolerant and catholic attitude toward the nuances of the gospel witnessed to in the ancient symbols of the Apostles' Creed. It testifies to the presence of grace in the ordinary circumstances of life, however extraordinary the experience of that presence may be. As a system it assumes that the new creation in Christ is present to the world in the Church, that the members of the Church are to be constantly nurtured in the understanding of that reality by disciplined reflection on the doctrinal implications of the Incarnation, but especially by living in the mystical presence of Christ through the Eucharist.

Publication of *The Anxious Bench* was followed in 1845 by Nevin's translation of the inaugural lecture of his new colleague, Philip Schaff. The latter's *Principle of Protestantism* appeared with an introduction by Nevin and appended the latter's sermon on "Catholic Unity" delivered at the Triennial Convention of the German and Dutch Reformed Churches in Harrisburg in 1844. He maintained,

The life of Christ in the Church, in the first place, is inward and invisible. But to be real it must also become outward. The salvation of the individual believer is not complete till the body is transfigured and made glorious, as well as the soul; and as it respects the whole nature of man from the commencement, it can never go forward at all except by a union of the outward and inward at every point of its progress. . . . [O]utward forms without inward life can have no saving force. But neither can inward life be maintained, on the other hand, without outward forms.[34]

The statement took issue with Protestant sectarianism and papal pretension yet maintained the necessity for a unity in time (history) as well as space. It was a statement threatening to the course of both popular and erudite thinking because its ideas were not unequivocally opposed to the truth of Christianity present in the centuries before the Reformation and it lamented the walls of partition so characteristic of American sectarianism. "If sects as they now appear," he stated, "have been the necessary fruitage of the Reformation, then must we say that the Reformation, being as we hold it to be from God, has not yet been conducted towards its legitimate results."[35]

In this sermon we recognize a further stage in the development of Nevin's thought, moving as it does from inward dissatisfaction with the emerging disposition of American religion to a search for an objective and historical context in which to resolve the intellectual dilemma. At the same time, his thinking is very much a response to public circumstance and not "art for art's sake"—theology for theology's sake. The thought of John Nevin may readily be characterized as a form of philosophical idealism, Platonic as it appears in its constant reference to an ideal form and influenced as it was by German ideas, particularly those of Hegel. Yet there is in it also a kind of social existentialism in which reality is a social and material phenomenon that must be inwardly affirmed and lifted up.

The sermon on "Catholic Unity" was followed in 1846 by what is probably Nevin's greatest work, *The Mystical Presence*. In it we observe the appearance of two categories that become central to his thought. "Mystical" is a word that has been the source of considerable misunderstanding, often opposed by orthodox thought as being pantheistic and the work of the Evil One, and relegated to the void of fuzziness and sentimentality by the secularist mentality. For Nevin, as we shall see later, the term had a very profound and intellectual use, as did the word "union." The life and work of Jesus Christ is a participation in the life of the world that effects a new birth in which we all may share. There is a union, an incorporation into Christ, that also forms the life of Christ in the human. Here is an idea that approaches the concept of theosis and deification so central to Eastern Christianity.

The Mystical Presence is a work of sacramental theology, the effect of which is to place its author farther outside the mainstream of orthodox Protantism and the popular Evangelicalism of the times. For Nevin is in effect affirming the notion that the meaning of Christianity is enacted at the celebration of the Eucharist. The union with Christ is not merely moral, or intentional, or remembered; it is substantial, real—a mystical presence. We receive in the Eucharist Christ's Body and Blood, not "after a corporal and carnal manner" but nevertheless substantially feeding upon Christ's life. Much of Protestantism had concluded that the efficacy of the Lord's Supper was dependent on the faith of the believer, that it was ineffectual apart from the Word of God in Scripture and preaching, or that it was a simple memorial rite. Nevin's ideas seemed more and more like the Roman Catholicism whose sacramentalism and papalism he professed to oppose.

Subtitled "A Vindication of the Reformed or Calvinistic Doctrine of the Holy Eucharist," *The Mystical Presence* directed its readers away from the Calvinism of the predestinarian decrees toward the mystical union implied in Calvin's insistence on the "spiritual, real presence" of Christ's Body and Blood in the Eucharist. Nevin celebrated a much more amenable and compassionate John Calvin than the one who is ordinarily discussed either in orthodox Protestant circles or among the cultured despisers. Nevin sought to interpret the Reformed doctrine of the Eucharist in order to make it more objective, historical, and catholic than Roman, Lutheran, or Anglican teaching on the subject. For Nevin himself, *The Mystical Presence* was a further advance in his personal struggle with the dialectic of the inward and outward: "The more intensely *spiritual* any state may be, the more irresistibly urgent will be found its tendency to clothe itself, and make itself complete, in a suitable external form."[36] He could relate such a statement as this to his own condition because the Reformed master, Calvin himself, had said:

> They are preposterous who allow in this matter nothing more, than that they have been able to reach with the measure of their understanding. When they deny that the flesh and blood of Christ are exhibited to us in the Holy Supper, *Define the mode, they say, or you will not convince us.* But as for myself, I am filled with amazement at the greatness of the mystery. Nor am I ashamed, with Paul, to confess in admiration my own experience. For how much better is that, than to extenuate with my carnal sense what the apostle pronounces a high mystery.[37]

A year after the publication of *The Mystical Presence,* there appeared *History and Genius of the Heidelberg Catechism* in celebration of the centenary of the German Reformed Church in this country. The book was an outgrowth of essays Nevin had prepared for the *Weekly Messenger* of the denomination in 1841 and 1842. He states in the preface that "the old material [was] taken up, with the addition of a good deal that is new, into a much more thorough and complete form."[38] Nevin's attention to the catechism is in keeping with his intention to revive the threatened neglect of the catechism in an unchurchly and revivalistic America. Already in *The Anxious Bench* he had advocated the "catechetical system" as an antidote to the immediatism and simplistic salvationism of Finneyian revivalism. The idea and use of the catechism was for

Nevin an important outward manifestation of the spirit of Christ in the world, the means by which we are instructed and nurtured throughout life and protected from the pride of inward self-satisfaction.

Nevin provides a very irenic portrayal of the Heidelberg Catechism as representative of a middle-way catholicism, moderating and mediating between the confessional extremes of Augsburg and Westminster, on the one hand, and Trent on the other. Based as it was on the symbolic structure of the Apostles' Creed, the catechism sought to avoid the pitfalls of those who define doctrine in order to exclude, who will not "confess in admiration their own ignorance" before the greatness of mystery. "All great truths," he wrote, "indeed are polar; comprise in themselves opposite forces or powers, whose very contradiction is found to be necessary at last to the everlasting harmony of their constitution. The catechism . . . is willing to tolerate *such* contradictions; and does so in fact. Its orthodoxy is not necessarily that of the Belgic [Synod of Dort] Confession."[39] It might be said that Nevin's thought was working at a vast mural in which the many features of "mystical union" were being depicted. His reasoning was systematic in relationship to various issues encountered in the public domain of American religion and culture. Every issue posed the necessity for some reconciliation of the inner truth of Christian faith with the outward circumstances of existence.

Three other major works appeared during the Mercersburg years. One was a sermon, "The Church," delivered at the opening of the synod of the Church convened at Carlisle on October 15, 1846, and published the following year. He wanted to be certain that the German Church in America had a clear understanding of the Church as an extension of mystical union. The Church was greater than the sum of its parts. It is an objective reality—"a real, supernatural, life-bearing constitution in the world." This is again a statement contending with the "rampant individualism" and calling for faithfulness "to the Catholic side of the Reformation." The greater danger to Christianity in this country is not "Romanism and Puseyism" but the spirit of sect and schism.[40] In the first volume of the *Mercersburg Review,* published in 1849, there appeared a two-part essay entitled "The Sect System" in which Nevin followed through with his diatribe against this radical American departure from authentic catholic Christianity, this critical ailment affecting American religion.[41] The articles were occasioned by response to the publication of a history of religious denominations in the United States by John Winebrenner. To Nevin the latter's book was not a history but a "literary salmagundi" of misrepresentation and sectarian special pleading. The year before these essays appeared in the *Review,* Nevin had published another work in which sectarianism had replaced the papacy as Antichrist.[42] His concept of the Church as a new constitution of humanity present in the world in its wholeness led him to address Protestant distortions of the one universal historical Church.[43] His appreciation of catholicity was making him more sympathetic to Roman Catholicism than to the sectarian fragmentations of Protestantism. The mystical union of Christ and his Church was an inner realization calling for its completion in a more universal historical (external) form.

Another essay that appeared in the *Review* of 1849 suggests that Nevin was now ready to take seriously the significance of this new constitution *for the world*. Heretofore, the emphasis was on the Church—it was the Church that represented the mystical union. Concentration on the Church question had required a move away from the moral and ethical concerns of his Presbyterian days in Pittsburgh.

For Nevin the year 1848 was the time in which revolutions in Europe signaled the coming of age of the American Republic.[44] According to Nevin, America must be careful that its propensity for individualism and self-interest does not become a New World nationalism that is an extension of the same principle at work in utilitarian individualism, merely the collectivization of individual judgments and aspirations. History presents evidence of Providence working toward catholic wholeness. The world itself is "wrestling" in its own inmost constitution, through the medium of American influence, toward a general and common end, which may be said to enhance the sense of its *whole* history for centuries past.[45] Here we see two of Nevin's primary intellectual interests coming together. The Church question and the mystical union are seen in relationship to his concern for the philosophy of history. Nevin never completely resolved this issue, but it was a keen interest. Much of his later teaching at Franklin and Marshall College in Lancaster dealt with the philosophy of history. Perhaps he failed to understand sufficiently that there may be a sense in which not just Christ and the *believer* are one, but that the *world* has its life from Christ. Perhaps Nevin's thought was still too much controlled by Reformation paradigms, too religiously concentrated on what are called believers and belief. The significance of Christianity may well be found in its philosophy of history, not in a salvationism that nourishes believers. What Will Herberg has said of Americans has been true of the most intellectually sophisticated as well as the rest of us: "Of course, religious Americans speak of God and Christ, but what they seem to regard as really redemptive is primarily religion, the 'positive' attitude of believing."[46] Nevin had realized this himself as early as *The Anxious Bench,* where he criticizes "new measures" revivalism because it assumes that religion does not get the sinner, but the sinner "gets religion." The subjectivity of religion, he had pointed out, is not created by its subject or from its subject. Justification is *by* faith, not by feel-

ing.[47] But it is just here that the problem lies—faith is confused with believing, and together they are usually transmuted into concern for redemption
as a human action. To this issue we shall return.

As Nevin went into retirement in 1852, he turned his attentions again to
a study of catholicity. He probed the ancient creeds and the early church
fathers and looked with renewed interest at the Oxford Movement. "The
Anglican crisis" of the times, he contended, was evidence of the centrality of
the Church question because, in England, the Church's freedom to interpret
the teachings of its own historical development was hampered by the state.
And Anglicanism's attempt to devise a vindication of a supposed pristine catholicity that had existed during the days before papal imperialism was to Nevin
little better than Anabaptist pretensions about the purity of the first four centuries. The anti-Romanism of Anglican polemics was without warrant. Nevin
came to the conclusion that it is historically and theologically impossible to
understand the reality of Roman Catholic development except as an essential
aspect of Christianity itself. His articles "The Anglican Crisis," "Early Christianity," "Cyprian," and "Catholicism" were published in the *Mercersburg Review* during 1851 and 1852, just at the time of his retirement from his office
at Marshall College and the theological seminary in Mercersburg. They reveal
the crisis in his own thinking, his own life:

> No opposition to Romanism can deserve respect, or carry with it any true
> weight, which is not based on some proper sense of its historical relations to
> early Christianity and to modern Protestantism, in the view now stated.
> Without this qualification, anti-popery becomes altogether negative and de-
> structional toward the Roman Church, and is simply blind unhistorical radi-
> calism. . . . Its war with Romanism is a rude profane assault in truth upon
> all ecclesiastical antiquity.[48]

Nevin had debated with Charles Hodge of Princeton about the nature of
sacramentality and the Reformed doctrine of the Lord's Supper. He had challenged Orestes Brownson, well-known journalist and convert to Roman Catholicism, with a vision of Evangelical catholicism that he shared as more
sublime and catholic than Roman Catholic authoritarianism.[49] Many in the
German Reformed Church (indeed, in much of American Protestantism, inasmuch as Nevin's views had become widespread) had become uneasy with
what they considered his flirtations with Canterbury and Rome. And, indeed,
in a letter of February 26, 1853, to J. A. McMaster of New York, he acknowledged the forwarding of a letter from Archbishop John Hughes. He informed
McMaster, who edited the *Freeman's Journal,* of his intention to reply to
Hughes. Apparently there were those in the Roman Church who eagerly

awaited Nevin's conversion. "Meditation and prayer," he wrote, "rather than any dialectic process, must bring to a solution at last the great problem with which I feel myself confronted here now every day."[50]

Nevin was very much a polemicist in the public arena of American religion. He was often thought contentious and satirical. But his inner struggle with the outward circumstances of American religion and the essential external nature of the Church had brought him to the point where he informed McMaster that "controversy and debate in any ordinary form have come to be for me . . . of very little interest or force." There is too much error and confusion in the world to be confidently dogmatic in any position not upheld by tradition. He withdrew from his ecclesiastical and academic responsibilities in order to "deal with this great Catholic question, as independently as possible of all outward restraints. . . . Should it become necessary for me to take the step you anticipate, I shall have opposition enough from a wide system of private relations, aside from all public connections, to make it a species of moral martyrdom."[51]

John Nevin did not take that step. Too much of a sacrifice of inner freedom was involved, too much of a threat to that vision of the Catholic Church that would embrace the truth of the Reformed Catholicism of the sixteenth century and carry it into the future. His personal pilgrimage had set an intellectual agenda that would keep him busy through a retirement of eight years, until at the dawn of the Civil War he returned to the Department of History at Franklin and Marshall College. The war itself forced Nevin out of whatever interior retreat he had sought to enter. Retreats, left to themselves, do not permit any resolution of the human dilemma. They require a public encounter in order to be clothed properly in some external form.

Accordingly, Nevin's thought turned to the matter of history. He was asking, how shall we understand the events of the day, the crisis facing the Republic? Christ is no abstraction. He is the revelation of God's reconciling involvement in the temporal order. Temporal existence is history. Therefore, it becomes necessary to sort out the role of Christ's mystical union in the order of human events. It was not merely a matter of "applying" Christian teaching to the course of those events but of using the resources of the mind of Christ in order to understand what God is doing. The Church and its sacramental life must ever be nurturing that mind. "Christ is the central fact, from which all other historical facts derive their significance. He is the key that unlocks its mysteries and apparent contradictions."[52]

During his seclusion, Nevin had taken up issues of the Church year and the matter of liturgy. Both of these external forms were ways in which the "constitution of the world is sanctified, by being taken up into the constitution of grace."[53] They involved him in further controversy with many in American Protestantism who had resolved matters of worship in the same way they had dealt with the nature of the Church. What Nevin called the Puritan and Methodistical character of religion tries to set its worship above all outward forms and conditions. Such notions, he said, were unhistorical, falsely spiritual—"infected throughout with the old leaven of Gnosticism, which is, ever in disguise, again nothing else but the secret virus of Rationalism."[54] He was chair of the denomination's committee to revise the liturgy for more effective use in the churches. A provisional liturgy was presented in 1857, and a revision entitled *The Order of Worship for the Reformed Church in the United States* appeared in 1866. Opposition to the liturgy and its rationale occurred almost immediately, and Nevin published a *Vindication of the Revised Liturgy, Historical and Theological* in 1867. The *Vindication* reviews the work of preparation of the liturgy and justifies its existence on the basis of theological positions already identified as the Mercersburg Theology.

In 1866 John Nevin was prevailed upon to again assume the presidency of Franklin and Marshall College, then recently located in Lancaster, Pennsylvania. Here, in the bosom of our American Republic, he told the faculty and students in his lectures, a new era in the world is taking place. Here the issues of human rights, of self-government, social justice, race, material well-being, arts, and sciences are to be settled. Our nation is "world-historical" in significance. Here also we will settle the great ecclesiastical issues Christianity faces in a fragmented society. Here we shall see whether there is an order of grace in the world—the mystery proclaimed by the Creed in its article of the Church.[55]

It was a vigorous ultimatum, demonstrating the manner in which Nevin had come out of the theological quandary in which he had found himself after the Mercersburg years. He was convinced, of course, that the great temptation of the age, enamored as it was of scientific, technological, and industrial power, was to assume that the natural order, turned in upon itself and feeding upon itself, was sufficient to the task of human fulfillment. This was contrary to the truth of Christianity, which witnesses to the presence of a higher order than the natural life.

As he contemplated the role of education and the life of the Church in postbellum America, John Nevin was constantly aware of what he had called the "sublimated utilitarianism"[56] of American religion and the shortsightedness of humanitarianism. Education, he thought, is the development of the forces at work in the constitution of humanity directing it beyond the natural laws of mere physical growth. "Education is, in general terms," he wrote, "the development of man's ethical and spiritual being."[57] But education in this sense requires recognition of a world in which the individual self must be able to see itself as part of a general or universal existence. For this to take place there must be an openness to the constitution of grace. Education and true religion can never be individualistic, naturalistic, or separate.

Nevin remained in public life until his second retirement in 1876 at the age of seventy-three. There is little doubt that he had mellowed during the last twenty years of his life. Although he spoke to many of the same issues in addresses, sermons, and essays, he was more irenic, less concerned to vanquish his foes and refute their ideas. There was, for example, the pastoral side of him that turned in the direction of ex-president Buchanan, whose home, Wheatland, was close by the college. He and Buchanan became friends, and Nevin preached a sermon at the ex-president's funeral on June 4, 1868. To have known Buchanan, said Nevin, was to be bound to events of world-historical (a favorite phrase of Nevin's since 1861) significance.

There are those who make much of Nevin's attention to the work of Emanuel Swedenborg, thinking it represented an intellectual weakness or a kind of retreat into the mysteries of spiritualism, away from the ecclesiastical controversies of his earlier life. Nevin had been aware of Swedenborg's work all along. He had criticized it for its lack of distinction between natural and supernatural realms, its lack of theological precision. But John Nevin, like all those whose intellectual pursuits are bound together with the quest for self-understanding, had always had an eye for seeing the extraordinary in the ordinary. He once wrote:

> My own religion was constitutionally . . . of a mystical tendency and turn. . . . It is not necessary to say what exactly it amounted to in myself more than this, that there was in me a sense and feeling of much in Christianity which was not to be reached in the way of common thought; but needed for its discernment and apprehension a deeper and more vital mode of knowledge.[58]

As James Nichols points out, Nevin's investigation of early Christianity had changed his attitude toward much of the seemingly folk piety of Roman Catholicism. He had accepted the idea of prayers for the dead and the intercession of saints. There was an acknowledgment of the Church triumphant with which we share the communion of saints.[59] The spiritualization of Swedenborg seemed less astonishing when one realizes that Nevin experienced the death of two sons during his second tenure as president of Franklin and Marshall College.

He retired while still in vigorous health and lived for ten years beyond retirement until his death on June 6, 1886, in his eighty-fourth year. Theodore

Appel, Nevin's biographer, quotes Neander as saying: "The office of the historian, . . . like that of the painter, is to let the soul of man, the animating idea of his philosophy, stand out in prominent outlines. . . . The lofty mission of the historian is to recognize the divine impress in outward appearance and to develop this out of its temporary obscuration. . . ."[60] We have observed the prominent outline of the thought of John Williamson Nevin, seeking therein some animating idea. His entire career was devoted to recognizing "the divine impress in outward appearance." The philosophical idealism that undergirded his thinking was never a denial of the significance of the material order. His thought is a matter of artistry seeking to reveal the connection between the inward and outward aspects of existence as he struggled with the religious and cultural circumstances of the adolescent American Republic.

two

WHAT IS SYSTEMATIC THEOLOGY?

According to Nathan O. Hatch:

> Nevin saw this linking of the Bible with private judgment . . . as a quest for primitive or apostolic Christianity, an emphatic revolt against theological systems . . . and a practical rationalism that made the ultimate measure of Christianity consist in "the exercises of the single mind separately considered." [1]

Hatch reminds us that Americans "relished the right to shape their own faith and submit to the leaders of their own choosing." [2] The culture assaulted all mediating elites and institutions, and ignored tradition, structure, and history. The common people generated their own ideas and leadership. They were not especially enamored of education or hierarchical orders. Yet, of course, their democracy was a leveling sort of democracy in which an aristocratic impulse asserted itself among those who leveled in order to acquire power for themselves. [3] In some sense the thought of John Williamson Nevin is a reaction against what Hatch called "the democratization of American Christianity." Nevin deplored the lack of systematic analysis and constructive logic in American religious life. He foresaw what historian Richard Hofstadter was to characterize as the anti-intellectualism of American life. Hatch maintains the people have their own levels of theological discourse which elitists like Nevin, steeped in tradition and the Church's authority, find threatening and appalling.

It is true, of course, that the German Reformed Church, adopted theological home of John Nevin, had suffered a great deal at the hands of a democratic Evangelicalism that led Jacob Albright, Philip Otterbein, and John Winebrenner out of the struggling denomination into the formation of new forms of Nevin's "sect system." The publication of *The Anxious Bench* in 1843 and 1844 was a response to the revivalistic and sectarian erosion of the German Reformed Church. Perhaps Nevin had expected the German Church to be more resistant to the religious subjectivism he had deplored in his former home among the old school Presbyterians. After all, the German theology, philosophy, and history he was reading seemed to provide intellectual resources for attacking the false rationalism and individualism of the modern age. He knew that there was controversy in Germany itself between left-wing Hegelians and the high church Lutheran confessionalists. But he may have assumed that the German Reformed Church could be a mediating force, avoiding the extremes of American Evangelicalism and European romanticism. The German heritage could demonstrate the need for systematic thinking that is not mere scholasticism or positivistic orthodoxy. The German mind had begun to come to terms with history and the idea of organic development. These insights, allied to the intellectual needs of Christianity, could save the American Church from the ravages of sectarianism and subjectivism.

THEOLOGY AS CRITICISM

It has sometimes been suggested that John Nevin was not a systematic theologian, meaning, of course, that he constructed no self-contained system of doctrinal explication. Nichols has said that the Mercersburg Theology waited for a systematic theology until Emanuel Gerhart wrote his two-volume *Institutes of the Christian Religion*[4] in 1891–94. However, the work of theologians like John Nevin places a new question before the house of American Religion: What *is* systematic theology?

Philip Schaff's *Principle of Protestantism* represents the heart of Schaff's inaugural lecture to the chair of church history at Mercersburg. Prior to his lecture Schaff had heard Nevin's sermon entitled "Catholic Unity." There was so much in common between these statements that the two men knew they were in agreement about many things.[5] Americans, said Schaff, were concerned with practical issues and opposed theology as detrimental to living, practical piety. Even those who defended theology did so on utilitarian grounds—it was useful. But in this work Schaff suggested that theology is the result of years of thought and suffering. It is sound scholarship, which is more important than fluent rhetoric. The intellectual faculties of human beings are to be used in service to God. Superficial knowledge is irreligious, said Schaff. Faith itself employs reason in its evolution into knowledge. Ideas rule the world; theology is the pursuit of the ideas that are the very heart of Christianity. The Church must not countenance ignorance.[6]

Schaff's concern for theology was shared by Nevin. "By glancing at the list of articles [published by Nevin]," writes Luther Binkley, "we can discover that he rarely wrote a systematic statement of anything concerning the Church or theology without first investigating it from the historical point of view."[7] He was certainly an exponent of sound and systematic thinking. Systematic theology was not necessarily the construction of an integrated system of conceptual images sufficient unto itself. It was systematic reflection upon the human condition, utilizing the mind of Christ represented in the tradition. Systematic theology derives the insights of revelation from the study and interpretation of history; it thinks carefully about the natural world with a mind that transcends the natural order—a mind that is more than time and space presently conceived and experienced.

Nevin's theology is systematic but not positivistically systematic. His thinking is a significant departure from much of the American theology of his day. American theology often tended to be either the exposition of a scholastic system or the attempt to place Christian ideas in service to the need for an affirmation of subjective experience. That is to say, in the first instance, theology was done with the assumption that common sense made it possible for the system of Christian ideas about creation, sin, and salvation to be understood as ends in themselves. The Princeton theology of thinkers like Charles Hodge represented this end of the spectrum. To this style of theology might be added the strict confessionalism of some Lutherans. However, at the other end of the spectrum there could be found varieties of theologizing that sought to affirm the dominant American value of independent private judgment and a belief that the natural order could reveal whatever truth was essential to effective and practical living. From Nathaniel Taylor to Horace Bushnell, the theological paths showed evidence of the footfalls of human confidence in the near self-sufficiency of individual experience and practical reason. Even the thinking of Charles Finney affirmed the free responsibility of the individual will to take initiative in its own transformation.

THEOLOGY AS INCARNATIONAL THINKING

John Nevin's thinking is at odds with both these theological tendencies. First, it bears a certain affinity with the liberals (e.g., Taylor, Bushnell) *and* the Finneyites in its insistence that theology is historical work. By historical, in this context, I mean only to suggest a certain emphasis on human existence— the historical world. Nevin's understanding of historical responsibility is more sophisticated than that of either early liberalism or new measures revivalism. His thinking, however, does not bask in a mere positivism of revelation that holds itself as a self-contained truth system. Nevin takes very seriously the fact of Incarnation—God-with-us! He was fond of the principle set forth in a text from Matthew's Gospel: "Lo, I am *with you always,* even unto the end of the world" (Matt. 28:20; emphasis mine). "How utterly at war [is this] with the notion of a quickly apostatizing and totally failing church," wrote Nevin.[8] Christ is continuingly present *in the world.* His presence is a "with-you" presence, which is the Church enduring on its first foundation through all ages. Implicit in this idea is the sense of continuity and community that runs counter to the notions of American individualism. For much of Evangelicalism, liberal or conservative, there is the assumption that the Church is limited to an ideal realm of salvation or rationalistic moralism, which the individual affirms by decisive experience. The liberal will appropriate that experience as a set of principles to apply to the improvement of worldly conditions. But Nevin's theology rejects that assumption as sheer naturalism, which assumed that the natural circumstances of life in this world were sufficient unto themselves, requiring only nurture, guidance, and goodwill. This kind of theology did not take seriously the presence in the world of a new constitution of grace communicated in the sacramental life of the Church. Much of American theology was naturalistic and rationalistic, failing to understand the nature of *the Church.* And, of course, scholastic orthodoxy was frequently quite Gnostic in its view of the Church and its refusal to take seriously *the world* in which the Body of Christ is present.

A second way in which Nevin's thought was at odds with most American theology is related to the first: theology is not thinking *about* faith or revelation but thinking by *means* of it. It is not speculation from or upon ideas, but *thinking with* the mind of Christ. Therefore theology is not a matter of quest but assumes the presence of what is quested. Faith is an epistemological reality, an alliance of rational necessity with an awareness of its own participation in a relationship that is greater than our own natural ability to express or contain. Nevin's theology makes much of the mystical union:

> Religion does include knowledge as one of its elements; but to conceive of it as an intellectual phenomenon only, is to mistake its true life entirely. Its inmost nature is love and reverence, a pervading sense of dependence on God and communion with him. . . . If religion consisted in doctrine, it might be imparted fully, like logic or mathematics, in the way of definition and demonstration. But this is impossible.[9]

Nevin wished to go beyond even "supernaturalism and naturalism." Although we may find it necessary at times to use linguistic constructs like "natural" and "supernatural" in order to make rational distinctions, we must not suppose that we do any more than produce dogmas among other dogmas. The reality of the mystical union of Christ and humanity is beyond natural and supernatural, but it is present in the world in such a way that it forces us into doctrinal statements. Discussions of "natural" and "supernatural" are evidence of a truth that really holds such terms in dialectical balance even as it transcends them.

In effect, Nevin is rejecting the notion that theology is ideology. Theology may become an ideology, but it is not materially so. Ideology is a system of ideas, integrally formed in such a way that they require a total response. Ideologies tend to analyze a defective world and advocate a program of change according to system. Marxism is an ideology, and Michael Walzer informs us that Calvinism is more ideology than theology.[10] Ideology is a manifesto of ideas to be defended against all odds. Theology, in Nevin's sense of it, is religious thinking that transforms our very perception of reality. There is little doubt that much of what is called theology in our own day is either ideology or religious studies—the latter an examination and analysis of language about something.

Religious thinking with the mind of Christ is not sloppy, sentimental, or devotional thinking. It is systematic, careful thinking that is expressive of the mystery of what is known. Of course, every thinker worth the honor of his task must acknowledge that it is *what we know* that is mystery—the mystery is in the known, not in the unknown. However, the theological significance of this fact is usually left unexplored. Nevin, in his 1851 essay "Catholicism" (read "catholicity"),[11] makes it clear that this mystery to which all human culture points is clarified by the mystical union with Christ. The mind of Christ so masters the *inward* sense of every order of existence that it sets it "in full harmony with the deeper and broader law of its own presence." The significance of what is present in every thought and artifact of the natural world is raised to a higher order by the mind of Christ.[12] What humans aspire to in the natural order must be treated rigorously and honestly; otherwise there can be no revelation of the catholic significance to which it points. Great theology comes from those who reveal the greatness of the mysteries of existence—it comes from human greatness. Great people do great theology. In this context good theology is not good system but systematic and orderly expression of the mystical union of Christ and his Church, as a representation of what is going on in the world.

BEYOND MODERNITY AND RATIONALISM

The emergent modernity of Nevin's days had been fashioned by European aspirations and ideas that found a natural home in the setting of the new American Republic. The modern age was characterized by increased emphasis on subjectivity and trust in natural reason. Much theological reflection took its agenda from loyalty to a Cartesian sense of the relationship between reason and reality. As Loren Eiseley so effectively portrays the issue in his study of Francis Bacon:

> The worlds drawn out of nature are human worlds, and their imperfections stem essentially from human inability to choose intelligently among those contingent and intertwined roads which Bacon hoped would enhance our chances of making a proper and intelligent choice. Instead of regarding man as a corresponding problem, as Bacon's insight suggested, we chose, instead, to concentrate upon that natural world which he truthfully held to be pro-tean. . . . Although worlds can be drawn out of that maelstrom, they do not always serve the individual imprisoned within the substance of things.[13]

Bacon, the herald of modern science and philosopher for the modern world, had a much more catholic vision of human reason and its role in discovering the uses of life. He was not an advocate of the kind of subjective materialism and technology that was unleashed in the subsequent centuries. Yet, in many aspects, American thought (whether philosophical, theological, or technologi-cal) has been the servant of its own self-assured solecisms.

"For the history that I require and design," wrote Bacon in *The Parascene,* "special care is to be taken that it be of wide range and made to the measure of the universe. For the world is not to be narrowed till it will go into the understanding . . . but the understanding is to be expanded and opened till it can take in the image of the world."[14] Bacon was born in the middle of the sixteenth century, the Age of Reformation, in which was conceived also the very tendency that was to become dominant in the modern mind whether scientific, religious, or philosophical. That tendency is rationalism, an expres-sion of the atomistic mind, a form of subjectivism, according to John Nevin. Romanism may have sacrificed the rights of the individual to the authority of the Church, but it was Protestantism that was tempted to assert these rights at the cost of ignoring the significance of the problem of authority by subsuming it to egoistic proportions—thereby eliminating the issue entirely. The problem of authority in the modern world is an unresolved issue. Authority subjec-tively considered is atomism, anarchy, and absurdity.

Nevin's historical sense told him that in the sixteenth century the ten-dency to rationalism was still held in check by what I would call the catholic substance of the culture. In other words, the notion of subjective freedom still lived *in context.* There was still the likelihood of dialectical relationship be-tween authority and freedom. "The reason of the individual was required to bend to the idea of a divine revelation as something broader and more sure than itself."[15] In other words, the issue of subjective reason was worked out in responsible relation to tradition and the idea of truth as a transcending reality. Nevin followed Schaff in referring to sectarianism as practical subjectivism and to rationalism as theoretical subjectivism. Rationalism, whether theological or philosophical, was too spiritual "to make account of outward forms and services of any sort in religion," said Nevin. "All must be resolved into the exercises of the worshipper's own mind."[16] It is tempting to reflect on the manner in which Nevin's thought anticipated the ideas of twentieth-century thinkers like Ernst Cassirer, who reminds us that Plato recognized the individualistic limitations of Socratic inquiry. Although Cassirer's ideas may sometimes distort our understanding by their emphasis on social functionalism, they at least make us aware of the fact that humans engage in symbolic work that must be understood as a creative process that includes myths, rites and creeds, works of art, and scientific enterprise. The inference we make is that rationalism is presumptuous and solipsistic.

As Nevin wrote in his discussion of rationalism:

> The subjective is every thing; the objective next to nothing. Hence [in much rationalistic theology] the supernatural itself is made to sink into the form of the simply moral. The sacraments of course become signs, and signs *only*. Any power they may have is not to be found in *them*, but altogether in such use merely as a pious soul may be able to make of them, as *occasions* for quickening its own devout thoughts and feelings.[17]

Nevin's incarnational theology is clearly represented by his understanding of the Eucharist because, in the Eucharist, he apprehends the creative process in which the "real supernatural constitution unfolding itself historically in the world" is symbolically and objectively at work.[18]

Although much nineteenth-century theology was strongly influenced by modernism, John Nevin's own thought represented a reaction against those tendencies, as described earlier. The sense of history he had derived from the classical Christianity of his early life as an old school Presbyterian and that had been nurtured in the intellectual realms of German history, theology, and philosophy required an understanding of knowledge that resisted the presentation of both liberal and conservative American thinking. This resistance was active in Nevin's life from his days at Union College, where his "conversion" experience under the direction of Asahel Nettleton aroused an uneasiness about the value of his childhood education in church and home. Certainly by the time of the publication of his treatise against new measures revivalism, the systematic rejection of sectarian and rationalist claims was already in place. In *The Anxious Bench* he wrote:

> Both the ruin of man and his recovery rest in a ground which is beyond himself as an individual. If saved at all, he is to be saved by the force of a spiritual constitution established by God for the purpose, the provisions of which go far beyond the resources of his own will, and are expected to reach him, not so much through the measure of his own particular life, as by the medium of a more general life with which he has to be filled and animated from without.[19]

The true force and significance of the modern world were not to be found in its practical and theoretical subjectivism but in the potential for the expansion of understanding that modern science and philosophy represented. Only as human knowledge expanded toward the fullness of its own universal nature could it comprehend the fullness of the mystery of the Incarnation; and the latter mystery holds the key to understanding and realizing that fulfillment.[20] As a matter of fact, the course and end of the claims of modern science, philosophy, and humanitarianism are largely beyond, sometimes against, the sense and purpose of those engaged in these activities and their interpretation. It is essential for the individual to be responsible in the task of maintaining the dialectical balance between inward consciousness and the hosts of outward activity, both learned and routine, in which we are engaged. Failure to do this will bring disastrous results.[21]

THE CATECHISM AS THEOLOGICAL SYMBOL

Theology is systematic if it is a teacher in the style of the Heidelberg Catechism. The catechism represents the objective voice of historical Christianity, providing an epistemological magistracy that constantly urges private judgment to move beyond itself, to increase its awareness of the constitution of grace at work in the world. It is "in broad opposition to personal heart religion, as something fanatical, methodistical, and mean."[22] What Nevin called "Puritanism" and "Methodism" represented "justification by feeling" or subjective religion. The catechism had begun to be ignored in the American setting, especially as the result of Evangelical interests during the early decades of the century. Nevin acknowledged that it was tempting (especially in the face of the "moral resurrection" that took place under direction of the "benevolent empire") to ignore "the original character of the Church itself."[23] This inclination to affirm the present and the immediate was evident in American life from Jackson to Emerson. However, the German Reformed Church should be true to its heritage as a mediating and ecumenical witness to the development of catholic Christianity from earliest times.

The catechism, said Nevin, was the only "symbolical book acknowledged in the German Church." It was the rule and measure of the "public faith" and the basis of theological instruction in the university and the churches. Its symbolical character is represented in its refusal to define and to give answers that represent controversial statement. The catechism includes rather than excludes. It preserves and expresses those symbolic statements of Christian faith originally contained in the Apostles' Creed. "It is characterized," said Nevin, "by a sort of priestly solemnity and unction, which all are constrained to reverence and respect. In attending upon its instructions, we seem to listen to the voice of the Church, and not to the words of any single human teacher." [24]

The catechism becomes a model for systematic theology by organizing the symbolic content of the faith and passing it on without being caught up in party spirit. It does not represent abstract reflection, compiling a scheme or theory of the Christian faith for others to examine. "The Catechism is more than mere doctrine. It is doctrine apprehended and represented continually in the form of life." [25] It is the great merit of this document that it avoids polemics and excursions into metaphysics that confuse people. Such excursions may be necessary for the intellectual tasks of individual clarification or even communication, but they do not represent the symbolic content of the faith and may undermine the constitution of grace that is always catholic in spirit.

For Nevin the catechism emerges out of the religious life of the Church. It is the bearer of that life; therein is its symbolic authority. Symbolic authority is of "higher" authority than definitional authority, inasmuch as occasions of definition and confession arise out of symbolic empowerment. Symbol does not exist except by its apprehension in life. That is why the catechism is organized in such a way that it represents the story of human existence itself. The first part provides questions and answers about the human condition— what is called the misery of humankind. The second part sets forth the plan of human redemption, thereby presenting the doctrines and symbols central to the Christian dispensation, including the emphasis on the life of the Church as word and sacrament. The third part speaks of the thankful, moral, and prayerful life as response to our redemption.

There is a parallel between Nevin's appreciation of the theology of the catechism and his own theological agenda. External and objective doctrines have no force unless they elicit response from the inner life of the people. At the same time, the inner life requires the power of the outward and objective. The inner life cannot exist by itself because its true nature is not simply individual reflection or judgment. In a sense that same set of assumptions is at work in the catechism, where a kind of dialectic of correlation is at work between inner human necessity and the objective realities of salvation and Church.

The question-and-answer modality of the catechetical system is itself essentially one of correlation. Perhaps the modality is somewhat scholastically determined, so that when Nevin writes of the doctrine as apprehended and represented in the life of the Church, he forgets that it is an elite and not the folk who have determined what that life is. Nevertheless, question-and-answer is an attempt to give objective reality to the manner in which inward consciousness must come to terms with the symbolic content of the faith. Critics of the catechetical system accuse it of being unfriendly to the inner experience, to the occasional and ecstatic. Certainly the system takes more account of "the regular, the ordinary, and the general" than it does of the special. But, says Nevin, "[T]he extraordinary in this case however is found to stand *in* the ordinary, and grows forth from it without violence so as to bear the same character of natural and free power." [26] The understanding of the ecstatic and subjective experience places it in creative context, whereby the inner life has meaning only as it relates to the objective living union with Christ in his body. "Great purposes and great efforts appear only when the sense of the general overpowers the sense of the particular." [27] The life of mystical union with Christ is not "the property of a particular *self* [but] rather . . . a more general power in which every such particular self is required to lose itself. . . . '[O]ld things pass away and all things become new.' " [28] Nevin's theology here reveals a sophistication quite beyond its time. Although he would not have understood it so, there is a sense in which it offers to dialogue with a Buddhism that insists on the necessity of transcending the experience of ordinary, particular selfhood.

TOWARD AN APPOSITIONAL METAPHYSICS

Nevin's thought is a systematic attempt to transcend the philosophical distinction between essence and existence. The essentialist makes an ontological claim about the prior reality of an essence, a mode of being that is fundamental to everything and is expressed in particular forms. The existentialist insists that there is no prior essence, that reality is the assertion of particularity. It is difficult to resolve the resulting dilemma on the ontological level. That is to say, the arguments over essence or existence as the fundamental mode of being yield only to the development of party spirit or the self-satisfaction of effective debate. On the experiential level, we know that our judgments about the worth of any human venture are likely to be based on an image of what that venture *should* be or accomplish. The human imagination is the prior element in our consciousness. It is not so much concerned with modes of being (ontology) as with organizing the mind and our actions in some meaningful direction. Life is not an ontological reality but a performative reality. We live as creatures aware of participating in a mystery that sustains us but is never reducible to our desire to control it by rationality or regulation; our participation is performance, an enactment of mystery. That notion is certainly central to the thought of John Nevin.

I would suggest, therefore, that his thinking is appositional. The appositional posture is aware of the inability to resolve the ontological dilemma. In some sense it disregards the issues because it recognizes that reality is always prior to our assessment of it. How else could we continue living when our most successful arguments are turned away by equally successful refutations? Reality depends neither on my existential affirmations nor on my insistence on an absolute, an identifiable essence. It is encountered as a mystery to which the only available response is imagination, which is the *source of our rationality* and our action. This may be termed appositional because it is a reasoned attempt to give language to the fact that life is a response to a reality that is contextual. We exist in relation to a vast context of mystery that shares itself with us, defining and providing us with signposts for our imaginations. An appositional view of reality is aware of the otherness in which we exist, that gives itself in apposition to our imaginative needs.

There are times when we stand exhausted by our best efforts to explain or manipulate our lives. Perhaps we are even helpless for a moment. Our self-power has run its course. We become almost like a person who has suffered for a long time under some debilitating and incurable disease, who turns to his loved ones and says, "Let me go!" Yet often that moment of the discovery of the inadequacy of self-power is only an end to the self we *thought* we were. Sometimes we begin to smile in the midst of our discovery. We trust life even though it does not yield to our conditions of trust. We trust it because it is apposite! It is other-power! Life *really is* other-power, power that shares itself. That is often a world-shattering discovery. *Webster's New World Dictionary* defines the apposite as that which is side by side, a side-by-sideness that explains and makes the situation appropriate, suited to its purpose. We know who we are, learn to accept life, when we realize that it is other-power, sharing itself in mystery. It is never what we want it to be in the exercise of our self-power. It is not ideal or existential but appositional—the domain of other-power.

Although John Nevin did not use this terminology in order to facilitate his theology, there is little doubt that it represents a controlling principle in his attempt to think critically and systematically about existence. His imagination moved to find those logical sequences and images that could best interpret and make reasonable sense of the appositional mystery. In *The Anxious Bench* Nevin wrote:

> The life of the soul must stand in *something beyond itself*. Religion involves the will; but not as self-will, affecting to be its own ground and centre. Religion involves feeling; but it is not comprehended in this as its principle. . . . The restoration to be real, must begin *beyond* the individual. . . . The sinner is saved then by a living union with Christ [which] constitutes a new life, the ground of which is not in the particular subject of it at all. . . . The particular subject lives, not properly speaking in the acts of his own will . . . but in the power of a vast generic life that is wholly beyond his will. . . . Religion in this form becomes strictly a life, the life of God in the soul.[29]

Obviously, Nevin had already devised an appositional basis for doing theology by the time he was called upon to respond to the inroads of new measures revivalism in the German Reformed Church. The material for *The Anxious Bench* had apparently been worked over in lectures to the students at the seminary in Mercersburg and in response to the appearance of a new measures clergyman as candidate for the pastorate of Trinity Church at the foot of the hill, next to the campus of the denomination's educational institutions.

The appositional foundation of Nevin's thought is clearly evident in *The Mystical Presence*. In the appositional, as the domain of other-power, there is no implication of the dissolution of the self. Rather, the self is reconstituted. So, for Nevin, the mystical union with Christ is a dialectical process—"The soul [read self] to be complete to develop itself at all as a soul, must externalize itself, throw itself out in space; and this externalization is the body."[30] As we have discussed it previously, inner and outer always exist in relation to each other. Here Nevin is objecting to the abstract separation of soul and body, "which has come to be so widely admitted into the religious views of the *modern* world."[31] As Glenn Hewitt suggests, the discussion reveals an interesting understanding of personality that is appositional in character.[32] According to Hewitt's interpretation of Nevin, "Salvation—the *re-union* of will and understanding—is not possible from within; it must come from God."[33] In other words, salvation is the realization of apposition—the awareness of the inadequacy of ordinary self-power that is actualized only by the reality of other-power. This is who and what Christ is, the mystical union of inner and outer, self and other, human and divine. "We not only spring from Christ," said Nevin, "so far as our new life is concerned, but stand in him perpetually also as our ever living and ever present root. His *Person* is thus the actual bearer of *our* persons. And yet that is no mixture, or flowing of one into the other, *as individually* viewed."[34] This means that Nevin's understanding of the individual cannot be individualistic. It seems that Nevin is not always consistent on this point. His Protestant emphasis on the believer sometimes gets in the way of his historical understanding of personality as mystical union with Christ. Thus, Hewitt interprets Nevin:

> A life of holiness can be cultivated only as *the Christian believer* comes into ever greater dependence on the life of Christ *within*. It is the introduction of the life of Christ *in the believer* that marks regeneration. It is the growth of the life of Christ *within the believer* that marks morality. . . . Regeneration is like the planting of a seed in the core of an *individual*.[35]

Presumably Nevin's thought would require a paraphrase so as not to mislead the modern American reader:

> A life of holiness is cultivated as the life of Christ becomes ever more evident in the world. It is the introduction of the life of Christ, which exists in mystical union with humankind, that marks regeneration. It is the growth of consciousness of the mystical union among humans that marks morality. Regeneration is like the planting of a seed in the garden of humankind. Individuality is the consciousness of a mystical union that includes the other.

Unfortunately, this reconstruction of theology is not always clear to Nevin himself, at least as I read him. Yet I would maintain that it is consistent with the heart and systematic direction of his thought. As Hewitt himself suggests, Nevin refuses to isolate human autonomy from divine will. Will and intellect are also united in human personality.[36] The individual is not what she thinks she is, which is an autonomous reality. But life is appositional—it exists by relationship to that which is *more than* our autonomous imagination, and shares itself with us. It is the dialectical relationship of will and intellect, inward and external, divine and human. Our thinking becomes philosophically and theologically shaped by the mystical union of Christ with humankind, a union that makes the Church the symbolic, sacramental organism that is more than an aggregate of individual believers and is ever at work in the world.

In a sermon of 1863, celebrating the tercentenary anniversary of the Heidelberg Catechism, John Nevin delivered a very Christological message that upholds Christ as the life of a regenerate humanity that offers "power of unity in space and continuity in time . . . the most comprehensive bond of [human] organization [a] new creation [that] shows itself wider, thus, than all distinctions . . . that belong to the old."[37] Written ten years after his first retirement and before his return to the presidency of Franklin and Marshall, the sermon may be more pastoral and Evangelical than we might expect from the prominent theologian, on the tricentennial occasion at Race Street Reformed Church in Philadelphia, but it reveals the consistency of Nevin's system. There is the persistent reference to Christ as the very embodiment of the appositional principle—Christ as symbolic reality, as Incarnation, as the gift to the human imagination for sorting out the direction of history.

THE INDIVIDUAL "SEPARATELY CONSIDERED"

It is interesting to explore this theme by reference to the images and expressions that occur repeatedly in Nevin's thought. One of these expressions is "the individual separately considered." The phrase appears countless times in Nevin's writings and obviously carries an idea that he found essential to his task. Nevin effectively made it clear that the individual *separately considered* was a distortion of anthropological wisdom and of Christian teaching. The phrase was meant to characterize not only the autonomous mentality of modernity but also the epistemological necessity of the dialectic of general and particular. Knowledge is appositional and selfhood is relational. New measures revivalism and the sect are the results of

> the *imagination* that this life is something that stands in the *individual separately taken,* the property of a particular self, rather than a more general power in which every such particular self is required to lose itself. . . . The particular subject lives, not properly speaking in the acts of his own will *separately considered,* but in the power of a vast generic life that lies wholly beyond his will, and has now begun to *manifest itself* through him as the law and type of his will itself as well as of his whole being.[38]

In *The Mystical Presence* the phrase "separately considered" or "separately taken" appears at least a dozen times.

Whether speaking of moral union, national life, elements of the Eucharist, or the life of Christ, Nevin uses the expression in order to emphasize the relational quality of all aspects of human existence. Moral union with Christ is more than private agreement with his moral program and imitation of or devotion to Christian "principles." Moral union as a consideration and decision of the individual separately taken is naive. Moral union takes place because of mystical union, "a common life, in virtue of which Christ and his people are one even before they become thus assimilated to his character."[39] Ideas and movements emerge historically not in some mechanical fashion but always relationally and contextually: "The Reformed Church, as distinguished from the Lutheran, cannot be said to have taken its rise in the person of any single man, or in the religious life of any particular country, *separately considered.*"[40]

This insight into the relational character of ideas and movements is applied to Nevin's understanding of America in his essay entitled "The Year 1848"[41] and in another, "The Nation's Second Birth,"[42] published in 1865. To Nevin, what America represented was not some New World nationalism, which is simply an extension of the same principle at work in the private subjectivism of American life. Nationalism of this variety is simply a collectivization of individual expectations. The rising national spirit was tempted to become a variety of the *individual separately considered.* Ours is not the perfect model for a state; we are what we are becoming to the extent that the inner resources of our lives are able to respond to the coaxing of a more universal order. "We are not so foolish as to conceive of this under the form of a simple triumph of our national spirit, as it now stands, over the social and political institutions of the old world. . . ."[43]

In discussing the mystical presence in the Eucharist, and in refutation of the ideas of transubstantiation or consubstantiation, Nevin reminds his readers that the presence "is not such as to identify the body of Christ in any way with sacramental symbols, *separately considered.* It is not bound to the bread and wine, but to the act of eating and drinking. . . ."[44] The particular and the individual find their meaning in relation to the general and universal significance of Christ's life, an objective reality to which Christians are bound in a very ordinary manner—eating and drinking.[45] According to Nevin, the truth of this has been affirmed by the tradition from earliest times. The Incarnation itself is the medium by which the divine life, the general and universal, finds its way into our personhood. Christian faith is not some esoteric wisdom, some phantom of the spirit. The humanity of Christ is appositional reality. "Christ's humanity is not his soul *separately taken;* just as little as it is his body *separately taken.*"[46] It is a mystical union of inward and outward; it is the *more than* in the midst of us, creating personhood.

CONSTITUTIONS OF NATURE AND GRACE

Nevin's use of such phrases as "Bible and private judgment," "actual and ideal," and "mystical union" also exemplifies his commitment to the reality of life as appositional mystery. Of especial interest in this regard is his use of the word "constitution." Certainly the term is not his invention, inasmuch as it was used by such thinkers as Joseph de Maistre in his *Essay on the Generative Principle of Political Constitutions.* The word has an organic meaning rather than a contractual or documentary sense. As such it has affinity with the common personal reference to one's "constitution"—the constituent whole of one's physical and spiritual being. Reviewing de Maistre's book in 1847, Orestes Brownson opposed the notion that humans can create a political constitution as they might a wheelbarrow. According to Brownson, de Maistre maintains that a political constitution is generated, not made. Any document that emerges is the formal principle of an inner, more organic constitution. The American Constitution is therefore the written document revealing the constitution, the living soul, of the nation.[47]

John Nevin uses the word to refer to the organic and constitutive character of human existence in the natural world, humanity in its otherness, its relatedness to the whole order of natural being. This allows him also to use the word in reference to the Incarnation, that mystical union with the world, which raises it beyond the natural order. The Church, the continuing manifestation of the mystical union, becomes the constitution of grace. The Church, like the Incarnation, "involves a regular advance undoubtedly from the outward to the more inward . . . the divine and the human, God and man . . . in the first place reconciled in its very constitution, as the ground of redemption for the race."[48] Existence is a mystery, a fact that is itself expressed by the manner in which the constitution of nature is known for what it truly is only in appositional relation to the constitution of grace.

When Nevin uses the terms "actual" and "ideal" to speak of the Church, he is reminding his hearers that the *actual* Church provides the opportunity, the structure or process, in which the new creation is actually experienced. The actual Church is never complete, it is not perfect or without error or sin—it is always more than it knows or realizes. The ideal Church is thus not an illusion or a whimsical expectation but an experienced reality in the midst of social structures that sometimes frustrate its realization but always bear witness to it. In some sense it is the experience of what Victor Turner calls *communitas,* which influences the social order both from below (as ritually conceived experience) and from above (as a ritually manifested ideal). It becomes appositionally present in its difference from society. It is "made evident or accessible . . . through its juxtaposition to, or hybridization with, aspects of social structure."[49] Here Turner's reference to "juxtaposition" is akin to the concept of apposition I have used in interpreting Nevin's thought. Certainly Nevin reaches for the same understanding when he writes of the Ideal Church as

> the power of a new supernatural creation [the "supernatural" is Turner's liminality so essential to the *experience* of *communitas*], which has been introduced into the actual history of the world by the incarnation of Jesus Christ.

. . . It is *a living system* [and] must be regarded in the nature of the case as the highest possible form of humanity itself; and in this view it cannot be less single or less comprehensive than the idea of the human race as a whole.[50]

THEOLOGY AS LIVING SYSTEM

It may be true that John Nevin "did not originate a system of thought"[51] if by system we mean a systematic structure that proceeds in logical sequence from one doctrinal image to another. However, because he understood the Church itself to be "a living system" in history, his life was devoted to systematic theological analysis and deconstruction of the religious, social, and cultural events of nineteenth-century America. Just as surely he reconstructed the "living system" in the light of historical consciousness and attention to the principle of the historical development of Christianity. His thought gives evidence of a remarkable consistency from his days at Mercersburg until his death in retirement in 1886. Although the pastoral circumstances and the personal agenda of his latter days may have mellowed the intellectual vigor of his earlier days, he replied to accusations of Germanizing in 1868: "The Christological principle has been for us immeasurably more than the requirements of any school of philosophy; its practical consequences have weighed more with us than the logical necessities of any metaphysical system."[52] In 1867 Isaac Dorner, celebrated professor of theology at the University of Berlin, wrote an article on the liturgical controversy in the Reformed Church in the United States (German Reformed), which was published in the *Jahrbücher für deutsche Theologie.* In it Dorner sought to promote peace and conciliation in the American Church by calling attention to the nature of Mercersburg's departures from German theology. However, according to John Nevin, Dorner had permitted his Christology to stop short of coming to terms with the fullness of the Incarnation, resting instead on the Atonement and its apprehension by justifying faith. Perhaps Dorner did not give full systematic attention to the universal life of Christ, bound as he was in his theology by the shortcomings of the sixteenth century—particularly in Lutheranism.[53] Nevin did not wish "to follow strictly any German system or scheme of thought."[54]

In all this discussion, Nevin remains a very systematic theologian. Even in his latter days, contemplating as he did "the interior sense" and reflecting the notions that led critics to accuse him of Swedenborgianism, Nevin remained loyal to his systematic principles. He asserted the need to remember the objectivity of the "divine realities" celebrated by Christian faith. Their objectivity is experiential as well as ideational. Otherwise, "our faith itself, on which so much depends, becomes for us thus too often only a sort of talismanic rod to conjure with; while the doctrines we hold are found to be little better than a ghostly simulacrum simply of the high spiritual realities they are meant to express."[55] These thoughts in his essay "The Interior Sense," written in retirement toward the end of his life, are in some measure a restatement of what was maintained in *The Mystical Presence* thirty-some years earlier. What was essential is the "presence of the life and glory of Christ *as they are in themselves.*" Anything less is a hollow Christology with "power to lay waste the Christian system."[56]

David W. Noble, in his interesting study of representative American novels, writes: "It was proclaimed, in the United States in 1830, that every man had transcended the human condition to achieve perfect freedom in harmony with redemptive nature. Ironically, it was the thrust of romantic ideology in Europe which made possible this concept of American exceptionalism."[57] John Williamson Nevin opposed that romanticism in religion and in national self-understanding. He opposed it with a unique systematic exposition of the Incarnation in the continuing life of the Church in the world.

three

THE PUBLIC CHARACTER
OF THEOLOGY

One reads the following in an unsigned article published in the *Mercersburg Review:*

> German theologians, and German theology have their faults. Among these
> may be named the want of more close and living communion between the
> professors and the great body of the Church. . . . This gives a one-sided
> tendency to German theology, which we may hope to escape in this country.
> . . . The natural turn of the American mind [is] one of the conditions
> which will determine the character of American theology. . . . The pros-
> perity of the Church, the advancement of society, the purification and eleva-
> tion of public morals, will always enter as conditions into our theological
> science.[1]

Throughout the nineteenth century most American theologians had "close
and living communion" with "the great body of the Church." Ofttimes the pulpit itself was the forum for the development of theological issues, however te-
dious and inappropriate the practice may seem to us. As stated in the previous
chapter, theologians like John Nevin maintained that theology must be developed in relationship to the life of the Church in the world. Theology, according
to Nevin, was a very public affair. That assumption affected the character of his
systematic exposition of the Christian faith. His theology was directed toward
events and issues in the scholarly, social, political, and cultural life of the nation.
As a result, it was primarily apologetic, polemical, and frequently pastoral. Books
like *The Anxious Bench* and *The Mystical Presence* were responses to the circumstances of American religion and culture in their fascination with "the individual
separately considered." Extended studies published in the *Mercersburg Review,*

such as "Early Christianity," "Catholicism," and "Cyprian," may seem like academic precocity (art for art's sake, the thing studied because it exists); however, they exist in relation to Nevin's concern for a growing American intellectual and theological apathy. Nevin sought a way to demonstrate the importance of the Church and the movement of the Incarnation as they work themselves out in history.[2] Americans are ignoring something extremely important and are tempting the failure of their own great opportunity in the face of a beckoning Providence. Philip Schaff had stated, in *The Principle of Protestantism,* that theology is not "useful," that it is not a means to an end but the end in itself.[3] That is only true for Nevin in the most foundational sense of it—as the external, objective force of our thinking with the mind of Christ. However, in a very historical and developmental sense, his theology is *useful* intellectual engagement with the public mind.

In his extended review of Horace Bushnell's *Nature and the Supernatural,* Nevin bemoans the tendency of the age toward rationalism, which fosters a kind of infidelity that destroys Christianity by dragging it down into mere nature. This infidelity is very subtle and often unacknowledged.

> Our public life is full of such essential infidelity. It reigns in our politics. It has infected our universal literature. The periodical press floods the land with it every week. It makes a merit generally of being friendly to religion; but it is plain enough to see, that what it takes to be religion is something widely different from the old faith of the Gospel in its strictly supernatural form.[4]

We recognize here Nevin's interest in maintaining an appositional perception of existence as comprising a sharing in nature of a reality that is more than our knowledge of it. However, the thrust of the review of Bushnell is addressed to the public dimensions of the American age. He faults the educational system, the public schools, for promoting a one-dimensional view of reality that is in itself religion of a sort—natural religion, whether rationalist or romantic. There is that incarnational power in Christianity which requires of education that it "make earnest with the realities of a higher life in their own true and proper form."[5] The young will not be properly educated for the new age that hopes to dawn in the American Epoch; instead they will be taught to assume that they are fit "for the duties and trials of life, by holding their minds down to the things of the present world only, without any sort of reference to their highest destiny."[6]

RESPONSE TO THE PUBLIC AGENDA

Nevin's American and public theology turns again and again to the failure of perception, to the emerging truncated and one-dimensional character, of

American thought and action. The Civil War was a momentous occasion for reminding us of this fact. It was a world-historical event, not a mere national calamity. It was a great public moment, said Nevin, in which the nation was faced with a trial, testing us to see whether we are capable of rising above "our wholesale devotion to the interests of time and sense." We have been given a vision of the kingdom of God, but we are now under judgment to determine whether we shall follow the path of the perished nations of the past, guided in our instance by the index of leveling that reduces the kingdom to the orders of nature. "All created life, thrown upon itself and separated from God, must as a matter of course fall back upon the natural world in which it has its root."[7]

American theology, as the commentary that begins this chapter suggests, is a very public and pragmatic affair. To a great extent, American theology is public discourse, not ecclesiastical discourse. As the development of Nevin's thought indicates, theology is formed in response to cultural circumstances and events. It is not merely a form of sound words or of abstract reflections that compile a scheme or theory for some to look upon and study. It is incarnational thought, therefore public theology, public discourse.

Nevin's thought illustrates the character of a theology that is done in a company of strangers. The question we have faced since the beginning of Euro-American consciousness, and especially since the emergence of the Republic, is the Hebrew Psalmist's question: How shall the Lord's song be sung in a strange land, amid a company of strangers? The pluralism of our ideas and practices has been legion. The diversity of religion during the colonial era was partly the result of the elimination of restraint and the erosion of authority that occurred in sixteenth-century Europe. Emphasis on experience and individual response to *sola scriptura* had unleashed a deluge of religious claims and practices into the public domain. William Penn had already established the principles of American religion by 1677. A journal entry from Frankfurt reads:

> I dearly embrace and salute you all, in this day of the glorious fulfilling of His promises to His Church in the wilderness. For, He had reached unto us out, and brought salvation near us! For He hath found us out, and hath heard solitary cries, the deep mournful supplications of our bound spirits when we were as the dove without its mate, and the lonely pelican in the wilderness, when we were ready to cry out, Is there none to save, is there none to help?[8]

There he could relate the actions of divine Providence to the struggles and oppression of the people and project a millennial idea of the Church as the gathering of the saved in the American wilderness. Penn's Woods was to be haven for thousands whose "solitary cries" had been heard. The great number of religious movements of both sectarian and cultic varieties gave a distinctive character to colonial Pennsylvania. The experiential emphasis associated with Pietism yielded a strongly individualistic cast to religious practices. There were private individuals who saw themselves as the fullness of the Church. And, of course, the Unitas Fratrum of Count Nikolaus von Zinzendorf sought to be an agency of ecumenical union that would overcome the religious fragmentation, particularly among German-speaking Americans.

The Evangelical Alliance was established in 1848 in London, and a national branch was organized in the United States shortly thereafter. The original intention behind the alliance was to develop a coalition of Evangelical Protestant churches that would champion Christian unity and religious liberty. The alliance also marks the beginning of cooperative efforts against the unbelief and secularism of modernity and sought to wage a traditional Protestant battle against Roman Catholicism and "Romanizing" tendencies like the Oxford Movement in England. Klaus Penzel informs us that Philip Schaff at first opposed "the Evangelical Alliance as a narrowly Protestant, misguided ecumenical effort."[9] This was partly because of the movement's failure to acknowledge the developmental presence of the Church in the history of Roman Catholicism prior to the sixteenth century. The understanding of development, historicity, and catholicity shared by Schaff and Nevin during the 1840s and early 1850s would certainly have prevented an acceptance of the subjectivist inclinations behind the Evangelical Protestant agenda of the alliance.

According to Penzel, Schaff's attitude toward the Evangelical Alliance had changed by 1857.[10] We know that Schaff became more and more involved in ecumenical efforts as the century wore on. It is probably not too much to say that his Evangelical catholicism was gradually modified by the influences of theological liberalism and the concerns of biblical criticism. "By 1854," writes George Shriver, "he had stopped talking so much about American sectarianism and had started elaborating on healthy American denominationalism and the important role it would play in some kind of church union. . . ."[11] Schaff was becoming Americanized. From the time of his resignation from Mercersburg, he had been involved with interpreting America to Europe and increasingly engaged in historical scholarship that would provide the means for consensus in the "reunion of Christendom in the Creed of Christ."[12] As a professor at Union Theological Seminary in New York City and an active proponent of biblical revision, he lived in the mainstream of the liberal and ecumenical climate of the late nineteenth century.

PLURALISM AND PSEUDO-PROTESTANTISM

If it is impossible to understand the life and work of Philip Schaff outside of the context of American religious pluralism, it is equally true of John Nevin. However, Nevin's thought takes on a greater appreciation of the mystical union of Christ and the Church. Sixteen years Schaff's senior, Nevin was less enamored of the potential of American denominationalism and more concerned with the ability of America to rise above the materialism that made common cause with the subjective character of American nationalism. In 1845 he pointed out that the Antichrist was not to be identified with the papacy but was present in the sectarian spirit of "pseudo-Protestantism."[13] For Nevin much of the cooperative Christianity of his day was seriously flawed. Although denominationalism was an apparently necessary outgrowth of the Reformation, it was a temporary condition. This did not mean that ecumenical efforts could ignore the historical circumstances out of which differences had arisen. The restorationist movements such as the Campbellists had begun to act as irresponsibly as the Anabaptists in assuming that all denominational structure could be ignored in a "return" to the "simplicity" of a New Testament Church. Some five years before his retirement from Mercersburg, Nevin noted that modernist notions assumed that it was possible to arrive at a common understanding of basic religious beliefs without regard to a stable historical base of tradition and confession. The same was true of those Protestants who proposed a new federal ecclesiastical order based on a broad consequence of doctrine.[14]

The problem of what to do with a high doctrine of the Church and a sense of historical development in the light of the pluralism of American religion was an acute issue for the nineteenth century. We can almost decide that it was the central and shaping concern for the theological mandate of John Nevin. What we can say of the Church as the extension of the Incarnation or the constitution of grace in apposition to the constitution of nature must be justified in relation to the manifold claims of the many Christianities at work in the American setting. What does it mean to think that Christ is at work in the world, effecting the task of reconciliation and drawing all of being into a higher order that is the fulfillment of its own natural expectations? What does that mean when we observe a public life that is self-indulgent and devoid of transcendent reference? What does it mean when our church life reflects the same naturalistic bias as the culture at large, or else manifests sectarian fragmentation rather than unity? Indeed, how is the mystical union effective developmentally in the course of history when the evidence points to the growth of practical and theoretical subjectivism in the religious and secular orders? These are the questions Nevin was constantly addressing. They are public concerns that are uniquely characteristic of the American context.

THE RELIGIOUS LYRICISM OF EARLY AMERICAN DISCOURSE

Well into the twentieth century, it is possible to observe that American public discourse has been primarily lyrical in form. It has been expressed in a rhetoric that is concerned with motivation, hope, and providing a sense of common destiny among diverse ethnic and religious claims. Public address is important in the life of a republic because it has the assignment of reminding us that we are *e pluribus unum*. The language of unity, equality, and freedom constantly brings these qualities to pass by making them visible in the multifarious circumstances of the human condition. Unless the word is spoken effectively it will not become flesh. Public address cannot be factional. If it suits only the lives of some elements and groups within the culture, its rhetoric is ineffective. In these situations its public charter is called into question. Nevin's contemporary, the black abolitionist Frederick Douglass, reminded the nation of the dysfunctional character of its public discourse:

> While America is printing tracts and Bibles; sending missionaries abroad to convert the heathen; expending her money in various ways for the promotion of the Gospel in foreign lands, the slave not only lies forgotten—uncared for, but is trampled under foot by the very churches of the land. . . . The church-going bell and the auctioneer's bell chime in with each other; the pulpit and the auctioneer's block stand in the same neighborhood; while the blood-stained gold goes to support the pulpit, the pulpit covers the infernal business with the garb of Christianity.[15]

The pulpit, the lecture platform, and the political stump have all had a shared public role in American society and culture. Douglass understood that it was "*America* [that was] printing tracts and Bibles," that forms of Christian rhetoric served as the foundation of American self-understanding.

The lyricism of our public address is fashioned by the symbolic nature of both its origins in Evangelical Protestantism and its fundamentally religious purpose—that of providing a public faith. In reviewing Orestes Brownson's apology for his Romanism, Nevin takes his readers through Brownson's reasoning, acknowledging its inner logic:

> Where there is the infallible witness and interpreter of God's word, thus indispensable to the exercise of faith in what it reveals, to be sought and found[?]. It is not *reason,* whether as intuitive or discursive. It is not the *Bible;*

because this itself needs to be authenticated and interpreted by some infallible authority beyond itself. It is not *private illumination;* for that at best would give only a private faith, while what we are requiring to have is a *public faith* [emphasis mine], such as can be sustained by *public evidence* [emphasis mine], by arguments which are open to all and common to all.[16]

A truly public faith, according to Nevin, does not rest in an "outwardly super-natural revelation, transcending the whole order of our common life, and not needing nor allowing the activity of man himself, as an intelligent and free subject, to be the medium in any way of its presence and power."[17] Instead the higher order reveals itself through the very life and constitution of the public order, supernaturalizing it in the course of the historical development of that order.[18]

UTILITARIAN DESTRUCTION OF PUBLIC FAITH

A public faith is a highly symbolic reality because it must be based on more than the rational judgments and demands of its variegated constituency. It must be capable of fashioning and sustaining a "constitution." Symbolic language of this kind will be lyrical, possessing the quality of song and poetry.

Robert N. Bellah has sought to show us that a republic hangs together as a republic only so long as its covenant is renewed; that is to say, using John Nevin's language, only so long as the "constitution" of the American people is nourished by a renewed commitment and understanding "of an ultimate order of existence in which republican values and virtues make sense."[19] The American Republic, in this understanding of it, exists on a religious foundation. If the "constitution" is not nourished, the Constitution makes no sense.

Bellah and others have maintained that Evangelical Protestantism was the primary custodian and promoter of the national covenant and constitution. Certainly the Protestant leadership of nineteenth-century America also agreed with that judgment. Yet Bellah, from the perspective of the latter twentieth century, deplores what he calls utilitarian individualism as the source of our "broken covenant." He ascribes this individualism to Hobbes, suggesting that Hobbes had no transcendent reference other than the promotion of a common good through enlightened self-interest. Bellah interprets Hobbes as suggesting that the individual must seek what is useful, utilitarian, and to his own self-interest, realizing that self-interest will be unmanageable unless it remembers that it cannot unlawfully run roughshod over the self-interest of others. Hobbesian "utilitarian individualism" is understood by Bellah to lead eventually to the erosion of what Nevin referred to as the constitution of the Republic, a constitution that will stand only so long as the people love it and are nurtured by the judgment and symbolic encouragement provided by transcendent virtue.

There were those, like John Nevin, who understood the character of Evangelical Protestantism somewhat differently from Bellah. "Our very spirituality itself," said Nevin in 1861, calling upon the nation to understand the seriousness of the calamity facing it, "is too generally a sort of attenuated sensuousness—our religion a sublimated *utilitarianism*—our morality a nice calculation of profit and loss. The notions of gain and godliness are apt to run wonderfully together in our minds."[20] Seventeen years after the publication of the revised version of *The Anxious Bench,* Nevin was ready to speak in general terms of our utilitarianism, not confining his judgment to new measures revivalism. Revivalism was evidently a symptom of the utilitarian individualism that was winning the allegiance of most Americans. As it was with our "material, mechanical, commercial, poltico-economical interests," so it was with our spirituality and our religion. Evangelical Protestantism had itself become religious self-interest, an expression of the practical and rationalistic subjectivism that governed our public life. The notions of "Bible and private judgment" had their counterpart in the rest of the utilitarian individualism of America. Our religion was a contributor *to* and a reflection *of* that "maximization of self-interest" that eventually led to the breaking of Bellah's American covenant.[21]

LYRICISM AND THE MYSTICAL UNION

Nevin would have reminded Bellah that his "custodian" of the spiritual constitution of the Republic was indeed its *patron*. It was Protestantism bathed in sectarianism and a message that was without an understanding of history or a word of hope beyond what individuals could fashion out of their own private experience. Speech about hope, writes Walter Brueggemann,

> cannot be explanatory and scientifically argumentative; rather, it must be *lyrical* in the sense that it touches the hopeless. . . . [S]peech about hope must be primarily theological, which is to say that it must be in the language of a covenant between a personal God and a community. Promise belongs to the world of trusting speech and faithful listening. It will not be reduced to the "cool" language of philosophy or the private discourse of psychology. . . . This urging to bring hope to public expression . . . is premised on the capacity to *evoke* and bring to expression the hope that is within us . . . and among us. . . .[22]

The lyrical speech, according to John Nevin, is the language of the mystical presence, of mystical union; it is hope brought to public expression by the life of Church in its liturgy and its sacraments. It is language about "a covenant between a personal God and a community" that is greater than the sum of its parts, of a reality that is more than private individuals separately or collectively considered. "How could the words, *I am the Light of the World,* have any meaning," asked Nevin, "if after all there were some other light beyond this, by which we must in the first place be able to prove its own presence?"[23] Lyrical speech, like "I am the Light of the Word," is first-order speech, language recognizing the priority of the appositional character of reality. It is the appositional power of speech that has meaning which sets the tone for all rational and dispositional experience. As Nevin implies, there is no light for the world that can be judged by light already presumed to be present in the natural order of things. The light that is *in* the world by its own "presumptuous self-trust" must become aware of its own darkness—as in Plato's cave.

Only lyrical speech of a highly symbolic order can effect that transformation. It is the language of creeds and catechisms, which is not private reflection or ratiocination but *public* address. It is understood to produce images that have the power of detaching us from the worldly order of things in order to return us to the mundane as people of altered perspective. Presumably we see the world as it is rather than as our desires and expectations ordinarily frame it. These images and the speech by which they are communicated are public in the sense that they cannot be the creation or preserve of individuals separately considered. For John Nevin, the speech of American religion was in danger of losing its true theological significance by being reduced to the private domain of a false and pseudo-Protestantism. Only the catholic vision of historical Christianity present in the sacramental presence of the Church could maintain the power of lyrical speech and retain the public order of theology.

BEYOND ROMANISM AND UNITARIANISM

If we examine the broad contours of John Nevin's thought, we understand how it was shaped by the public character of American life. According to thinkers such as Nevin, we were confronted by the anti-Romanism of a Protestantism that was losing ground to the growth of Roman Catholicism. This was a public issue requiring theological address. We remember from his review of Brownson's Roman Catholic apologetics that Nevin thought Romanism betrayed the possibilities of public faith by imposing "a revelation of supernatural truth, which men are to receive by faith, as something wholly out of themselves, that is brought to them for their use in a pure outward way."[24] Faith in this sense of it is abstract, its authority refusing to engage the ordinary life of the world. Nevin was keenly aware of the fact that Brownson's apologetics sought to take the public order seriously. Like Nevin, Brownson was out to demonstrate the relevance of the Catholic vision to the social and political life of the American Republic. He, too, had a public understanding of theology but was unable to perceive the rationalistic dilemma of the Roman solution.[25] Brownson, too, wished to demonstrate the unsuitability of Protestantism in its subjective American guise to the task of maintaining the constitution of the Republic.[26] However, to Nevin, Brownson's Romanism was hindered by its loyalty to a "mechanical quasi-magical way" like a "supernatural automaton." Rather, according to Nevin, the Church is an event in the world, a gift of faith. In the creed, the reality of the Church *follows* the graceful reality that is Christ. "The Church is still necessary as an indefatigable witness to the truth; but her indefectibility is a moral fact, not a physical necessity, made good through the activity of the general Christian life itself, the life of Christ in his people, working out its own problem in a truly human way."[27] Faith is not to be separated from reason, acting only on abstract supernatural authority; rather, faith "opens to view . . . a higher form of what may be called its own proper life,"[28] which works itself out in our understanding by way of reason. The Church lives in the world as a mystical presence that illuminates the public dimensions of existence.

In the context of the American setting, "Unitarianism and Romanism are the contrary poles of Christianity, freedom and authority, the liberty of the individual subject and the binding force of the universal object, carried out each by violent disjunction from the other, into nerveless pantomime and sham."[29] This is an observation about the public character of the nation, an observation motivated by the need for theological response.

Here, in the midst of political circumstances where there is no establishment of religion, the problem of freedom and authority is exemplified in the dynamics of our pluralistic life. America is the field in which Unitarianism found a natural and conducive environment, emerging out of its conception in the humanistic Reformation and Puritanism. Here, also, the Roman Catholic Church is not the long-standing foundation of the European social and cultural order but must find a new articulation. America represents the deconstructive ground of modern history.

The humanistic perspective represented by Unitarianism is "of one measure with the natural life of man, because it adds nothing to this and has no power whatever to lift it into any higher sphere."[30] This perspective emphasizes the natural, the subjective and inward, at the expense of the outward initiative of the divine in the course of history and the organic life of the Church. In this manner the religious life does not grow but responds to the dictates of its own desire and understanding. On the other hand, Romanism results in outward and abstract conformity to the dictates of external authority.[31]

THE PUBLIC BUSINESS OF CHURCH AND STATE

Like many of the major thinkers of Europe in the mid–nineteenth century, Nevin struggled with the need for a valid understanding of the state in relationship to the development of Christian history since the fourth century C.E. For Nevin, however, the issues were pragmatic as well as theoretical. Metaphysical notions of the state, together with ecclesiological considerations expressive of a high Christology, had to find dialectical resolution in a public domain defined by the parameters of "no establishment of religion" expressed in the Constitution. Americans have always had to explore the meaning of "no establishment" in changing contexts. The meaning is not abstract or dogmatic (as some interpreters would make it) but situational and pragmatic. We have often continued to use the European jargon of Thomas Jefferson, with his repeated references to Church and state—a usage that has often been somewhat crippling, both of constitutional hermeneutics and of American public understanding.

The essential public question for America is: How shall the religious impulse be directed in a society wherein pluralistic claims often avoid responsible public expression because of institutional habits of exclusive behavior? "Congress shall make no law respecting an establishment of religion, or prohibiting the free exercise thereof"—that is the wording of the First Amendment to the U.S. Constitution. Although this may be interpreted using the static and exclusive language of European experience, our constant dependence on this latter language inhibits the free public exercise of religious thought and practice on behalf of the common good.

In his extended essay "Early Christianity," Nevin finds it necessary to respond to conceptions of the Church that were being addressed by German thinkers. He spoke out against the view of Richard Rothe of Heidelberg University, whose *Origins of the Christian Church* he was reported "to have described as the most stimulating book he had ever read."[32] Rothe claimed that the Church is destined to be assimilated by the state and as such will disappear. However, for Nevin the Church is no "merely provisional and transient fact." According to him,

Rothe's error lies in the assumption that the economy of the world naturally considered must be regarded as carrying in itself, from the beginning, all the necessary elements and conditions of a perfect humanity; in which view a real redemption must complete its work . . . keeping itself to the organism of earth where the law of sin and death now reign . . . instead of translating its subjects . . . over into some new and altogether different order of being.[33]

Nevin thought that the Church partakes of and incarnates a new order, a constitution of grace. It bears a radical catholicity, a wholeness that rejects all partial claims of truth and justice in behalf of an ever-inclusive raising up of the natural achievements and aspirations of humankind. No areas of life are outside the embrace of the Kingdom of God represented by the Church.[34] Therefore, the sacramental power of the Church must become a presence that grows more deeply so that the natural life of humanity is not divorced from the divine purpose.[35]

The state, therefore, is not outside the sphere of the sacramental mandate of the Church. "The imagination," said Nevin, "that the last answer to the great question of the right relation of the Church to the state, is to be found in any theory by which the one is set completely on the outside of the other must be counted essentially antichristian."[36] It is obvious, however, that no notion of Church as an established institution that excludes some dimension of public life is compatible with this theology. What the Church represents is the new constitution of grace that must constantly replenish the constitution of the public order represented by the state. The Church is embodied at all times in human institutions, but it is *more than* what is embodied. The self-sufficiency of *any* ecclesiastical system must come to an end (whether, for example, Roman or Protestant) as the radical catholicity of the Church moves to include an ever more universal reality.[37]

CHRISTIANITY AND THE PUBLIC ORDER

Much of nineteenth-century American religious thought was shaped as an adaptation to the need for appeal to potential converts. America was a nation in which the original constitution had been fashioned by the resourcefulness of clergy and laity engaged in securing a constituency and fashioning modes of personal piety. The landscape was sacralized by shrines that were characterized by simplicity. Churches were gathering places for assemblies of individuals who were to be auditors of a message directed at transforming them by eliciting testimonial evidence of saving faith.[38] Church buildings portrayed that assumption, and adjoining graveyards suggested that the passage from birth to death was ritualized in the context of the message of essential conversion. This image of visible sainthood was not confined to New England, with its attention to religious scrupulosity in the face of the uncertainties of divine election. Pietists, religious experimenters, and spiritual rationalists alike shared the compulsion to dedicate, to change, one's life. It was assumed that dedication was essential to the public order, that constituencies of dedicated people were essential to the common good. The result was an increased emphasis on moral distinction and private experience. "As a growing number of denominations competed for adherents in the free air of religious voluntarism," writes Patricia Bonomi, "points of theology proved less attractive to potential adherents than did a church's social program, the popular appeal of its preachers, or its geographical proximity."[39]

In the nineteenth century the forms of individual conversion and dedication found their focus in revivalism. However, the pattern of voluntary constituency, appeal to potential adherents, conversion, and dedication was already established. As historians like Bonomi and Jon Butler have shown us, there was little evidence of decline in religious identification; rather, there was a steady growth of diversity and institutional authority.[40] In this context the public dimension of religion was always in a state of flux. The tendency among Pietists and millenarians was to emphasize the primacy of inner devotion and otherworldly expectation. However, there is little evidence to support the hackneyed accusation of otherworldly apathy frequently directed at Christianity in general. Exponents of innerliness and millennial expectation used their religious resources to cope with the realities of *this world* and almost always developed programs of personal and social amelioration. The programs often relied on the moralistic assumption that dedication to simple private rules of behavior would confirm personal transformation and assure an appropriate preparation for the millennium.

Among those of more liberal and Enlightenment persuasions, the public dimension of religion also found varied interpretation. At one end of the spectrum were those like Jefferson and Madison, for whom religion would make its essential social contribution by being left to private resolve. However, even for these radical religionists, there was a religiousness that the "no-establishment-of-religion" clause would protect. At the other end of this spectrum were those who understood religion itself to be the imagination and formation of a peaceful kingdom. Altogether, American religion was to devise attitudes and assumptions that gave it a distinctly public shape. "Religion permeated early American life," writes Bonomi, "in part because religious institutions had to be built anew in the colonies, a task that incorporated the laity into the very fabric of the churches at the same time that it built the churches into the structure of civil society."[41] This development blurred the boundaries between religion and politics. It also guaranteed the blurring of theological distinction and refinement even when professional clergy espoused confessional principles. Much religious discourse has been at the same time public discourse and has served as the rhetorical model for political address, educational philosophy, and literary form and substance.

It should be clear from this discussion that the public character of American religion has always been partly an expression of the need for identity and social order. Many of the most adamant spokespersons for a "Christ Against Culture" or a "Christ and Culture in Paradox" model[42] of Christian faith were required to have some religious vision of the American purpose. It has not been easy for American religious thinkers to divorce themselves from the mandate to provide social order and stability. Today scholars of a postmodernist frame of reference may wish to remind us that all truth claims and religious traditions are socially constructed. However, most American thinkers, including theologians, have always been aware of the pragmatic task of religion in a virginal society.

From the standpoint of the history of religions, human religiousness struggles for more than experience, transformation, or healing. It seeks and expresses itself in cultural identity and social cohesion. Presumably this means that a religious tradition will work out some dialectical tension between the prophetic claims of personal insight and the socially controlling elements of the worldview. However, the blurring of boundaries in American religion has made this essential dialectic a difficult achievement indeed.

We can see this difficulty illustrated in the public theological career of John Nevin. Revivalism was the dominant public expression of early-nineteenth-century American religion, providing for personal transformation and for initiation into the mainstream of society. "Revivalism," writes Nancy Hardesty, "is essentially an American propaganda technique necessary in a society where religion has been disestablished and religious options are numerous." Yet the change from the religious pattern of colonial America was, as I have shown, not really so radical as might be assumed. "In eighteenth-century Puritan Massachusetts," continues Hardesty, "where all competing sects were banished to Rhode Island, church fathers could wait for people to get converted while still collecting their tithes."[43] Yet, as Bonomi and Butler have informed us, the effort to gain adherents and build a form of Christianity into the structure of the social order was present from the beginning.

The character of this American order of religion tended to be very moralistic and very protective of whatever social order had been achieved in so unstable and dynamic a history. We are aware of the recurrent phenomenon of "old lights–new lights," "old side–new side," and "old school–new school" in the history of eighteenth- and nineteenth-century Congregationalism and Presbyterianism. At issue in this continuing controversy is the relationship between religion as an agent of social *change* and religion as the foundation of social *order*. John Nevin appeared to the agents of *Anxious Bench* revivalism to be a defender of the status quo. As Hardesty and others have shown, the Finneyites against whom Nevin protested were in the forefront of the antislavery movement and the women's rights movement.

PUBLIC ORDER AND AMERICAN WOMEN

Old school Presbyterians tended to be very rational defenders of social order in the face of the "enthusiasm" of new measures revivalism which threatened to destroy the pattern of a society that had been centuries in the making. Women have a very important place in the scheme of creation and redemption, said conservative revivalists like Lyman Beecher. When Finneyites and eastern pastors met in New Lebanon, New York, in July 1827, "the two opposing camps managed to reach a compromise consensus on all issues except one: the practice of women praying aloud in mixed assemblies."[44] Many women were influenced by Charles Grandison Finney and found his interpretation of Christian perfection to be meaningful to their own experience. Phoebe Palmer, like Finney and the new school Presbyterians, emphasized the notion of the human ability to activate the will in accordance with God's will that we should be holy. Angelina Grimké credited Finney with providing a simple resolution of the problem of the nature of humanity and the requirements of God. Many women seemed intent on the absolute necessity of perfection and holiness as affirmations of what God has already made possible. Holiness became linked to the freedom of all humankind. Women who spoke on behalf of the abolition of black slavery found themselves speaking on their own behalf out of a recognition that God, indeed, made it all necessary and possible.

It is ironic that the conservative Evangelicalism and Fundamentalism that today attempt to preserve a moralistic version of social order are the direct heirs of Finney and his programs of holiness and social change. Why was John Nevin an opponent of Finney's new measures and his permissiveness with regard to women's rights, even though he shared the convictions of the antislavery movement? Nevin responded in highly traditionalistic manner to the fact that the "anxious bench" was very popular among "females and persons who are quite young." There is every reason to believe that he had a high regard for the educated and cultivated women of his day, yet he could not bring himself to disrupt the established order by having women engage in certain public activities or play roles other than as nurturers of the home as the microcosm of Christian civilization. We must remember that, as the mind and spirit of nineteenth-century America moved away from the stricture of Calvinist doctrines toward notions of human initiative and the perfection of humanity, the rhetoric of the nation was altered. Humans were essentially good, not depraved; they were capable of rebirth. Revivalism thrived on the rhetoric of rebirth, imaginatively subsidizing a female symbol.

Historians have shown us how the increasing absence of fathers from middle-class homes deprived boys of vital masculine models. Women became the redeemers of the nation, fixing into the character of boys "feminine sensibilities and identification with feminine roles."[45] Even Horace Bushnell's view of conversion, which Nevin found reasonable but insufficient, represented a gradual imbuement of God's spirit through maternal nurture. Mothers scorn all comparison with mere animals. The love of a mother

> looks through the body into the inborn personality of her child,—the man or woman to be . . . if she could sound her consciousness deeply enough, she would find . . . the call and equipment of God, for a work on the impressional and plastic age of a soul [which has] no will as yet of its own, that this motherhood may most certainly plant the angel in the man, uniting him to all heavenly goodness by predispositions from itself. . . . Nothing but this explains and measures the wonderful proportions of humanity.[46]

Although lacking in the freedom to participate in all of the aspects of *economic* and *political* life reserved for men, women became the shapers of American culture. "Middle-class women," writes Mark Carnes, "were not the passive victims of an ideology of domesticity, but the architects of a bifurcated gender system that elevated their status even as it circumscribed their actions to the home."[47]

The clergy were often the supporters of the values considered nurturing and feminine. They faced the stigma of effeminacy from those men who sought to solace their own loss of cultural effectiveness by engaging in male rituals that suppressed feminine characteristics and often coarsely effaced emotional ties associated with women. John Nevin supported those values that were fostered by the images of motherhood. He opposed the public role of women because he saw that change as a deterioration of the social order that reflected the virtues of Christian nurture. In *The Anxious Bench* he writes:

Nature itself may be said to teach us that woman cannot quit her sphere of relative subordination with regard to man without dishonoring herself and losing her proper strength. And it is no small argument for the divine origin of the gospel that while it teaches the *absolute personal equality of the sexes* as it had never been understood before, it still echoes, while it rightly interprets, the voice of nature with regard to this point.[48]

Unfortunately, Nevin's thought on the nature and role of women is largely undeveloped, except for his essay "The Moral Order of Sex" in the November 1850 issue of the *Mercersburg Review*. Given his objection to Bushnell's theology on the grounds that, for Bushnell, salvation and redemption occur entirely within the realm of nature and human potential, we might expect that Nevin would envision a transformation of the existing natural role of women. Instead he defends that role basically by reference to the "voice of nature"—*and* the Pauline authority. Suffice it to say, it is likely that Nevin accepts that Pauline authority not on textual grounds, which he would have maintained were subject to the vacillation of private judgment, but on the grounds of the necessity of the natural order as the context of revelation itself. Women are the reminder of the fact that our notions of equality are relative and conditioned by our natural myopia; they remind us also that the natural good requires the "raising up" that is fulfilled by the constitution of grace. Presumably he was unable to imagine that the constitution of grace, forming anew the Body of Christ, might have been at work in the sectarian idiosyncrasies of revivalism, raising up the natural good of women to new manifestations of public order. However, of that we cannot be certain even from the hindsight of a century and a half.

Before John Nevin came to Mercersburg, he had spent ten years in Pittsburgh as an advocate of temperance, a champion of a Sabbatarian Sunday, and an opponent of frivolity. Although he belonged to no antislavery society, he firmly believed that slavery was a vast moral evil. He was, in short, a supporter of much of the moralistic agenda of Finney, the revivalists, and the Evangelical Protestant established order. On the matter of slavery, however, he deplored factionalism, mean-spiritedness, apathy, and ideological warfare—all of it spawned in the context of this "vast moral evil."[49] But Nevin was not an activist, a joiner, a crusader. He decried "party spirit" and preferred to understand these momentous public issues as evidence of the onward movement of the Providence of God, providing the opportunity for humanity to internalize the outward signs of the coming Kingdom.[50]

four

A RADICAL AND REALIZED CATHOLICITY

The following passage appears in what may be Nevin's most remarkable and extraordinary article, namely, his essay of 1851 entitled "Catholicism":

> The universalness here affirmed must be taken to extend in the end, of course, over the limits of man's nature abstractly considered, to the physical constitution of the surrounding world . . . for the physical and moral are so bound together as a single whole in the organization of man's life, that the true and full redemption of this last would seem of itself to require a real . . . renovation also of the earth in its natural form. . . . Christianity is catholic . . . inasmuch as it forms the true and proper wholeness of mankind, the round and full symmetrical *cosmos* of humanity, within which only its individual manifestations can ever become complete. . . . Christianity . . . is catholic, as it carries in itself the power to take possession of the world both extensively and intensively. . . .[1]

In this passage we may observe the contours of a very interesting cultural theology. Nevin here suggests that Christianity, perhaps more accurately Christ as the Incarnation, represents the introduction of wholeness into the life of the world. The world can never again escape the fact that claims to truth are particular and partial realizations of a truth that is greater than the sum of its parts. Any claim to exclusiveness is inevitably challenged by the inclusive wholeness already present in "the earth in its natural form."

For Nevin Christianity was catholic in the sense that it represents the universal *in our midst,* already present, but judging and beckoning us to a more radical realization than is present among individuals, whether they are aware of it or not. This notion of "catholicism," which I prefer to label "catholicity," is, of course, somewhat informed by the Hegelian ideas that Nevin acquired from his reading of German thinkers. But, like much of Nevin's thought, it is generated and shaped by the American public context.

Nevin's thinking, I have maintained, was a very American enterprise. Understanding it involves a revised perception of systematic theology and attention to a pragmatic reconstruction of system itself. As American theology, Nevin's thought was also public, both in its response to the issues and circumstances of public life and in its concern that the religious assessment of humankind requires a public faith. What I have called Nevin's radical catholicity is also a response to the religious necessities of the American context. Radical catholicity is an expression of public faith.

NATURE POINTS TO ITS CATHOLIC SOUL

We must remember that, for America in the nineteenth century, the historical question was paramount. What is the direction and meaning of history in the light of the emergence of the American Republic? The millenarian thinking of many Americans like Joseph Smith, William Miller, or Ellen Gould White was spawned in circumstances of great frustration over the relentless change and unsettled conditions of American life. On the one hand, there seemed cause for optimism and the quest for perfection; on the other, there was no abiding rest. To many Americans, particularly among those dispossessed by the manipulators of progress or struggling with the techniques of survival, God was preparing the world for the demise of its sinful expectations and promising to fulfill history by way of the Second Advent.

The postmillennial mood of the other half of the American mind was encouraged by the growth of industrialism, the conquest of the continent, the discovery of gold, and the positivism of popular social Darwinism. To Nevin these were the signs of a revolution that was the dawn of a new historical period. The telegraph and the railroads were no accidents "in the economy of providence." They coincided with what he called "the completion of our American civilization" so essential to the circuiting of the globe, at which time "the end [is] brought round once more to the beginning."[2] A new age of universal history will have dawned. That which the present represents in expectation and in fulfillment of its past will be transcended. "The old movement [will not] be gone over again under a higher form." Instead,

The world will be brought so together as to leave no room farther for the idea of any such successional cycle. All betokens rather the abrogation of this law, as one that shall have finished its necessary course, by making room for the integration of all stages of the world's life ultimately into the conception of its proper *manhood,* as this is to be revealed in the new universalized culture, towards which so many signs are pointing and so many powers struggling at the present time.[3]

We may interpret Nevin as saying that the movement of history is in keeping with the providential ordering of existence in the direction of personalization—the "proper manhood" of the world's life as revealed in Jesus Christ. Christianity is, therefore, the new and transcendent conception of humanity, penetrating and transforming the world's life. This means that the true personhood, latent in the natural order of things, is coming to fulfillment. So far as I can tell, Nevin did not work through the implications of this idea in relation to other orders of being than the human, but the suggestion is certainly present. As a matter of fact, here is an agenda for contemporary theology, which needs to take more seriously the notion of *agency.* Scientific observation as well as artistic creativity cannot escape the instrumental source of their insights in the human personality—personhood is the *agency* of all our observation, measurement, and interpretation. Whatever is seen, thought, or postulated is dependent on the instrument of observation or thought—personhood, persons. When we become aware of the fact that *what* personality observes or creates is always more than its own capacity for final or absolute resolution or understanding, we have acknowledged the likelihood that personhood is characteristic of all of being, that the heart of reality is itself personal.

However, Nevin was the product of his time as well as a prophet of its extension into historical development. He was limited by the shared worldview of the mid–nineteenth century. He also knew, realistically, that "the life of our race as it now stands is in itself considered a profoundly fallen life; a life estranged from heaven, and from the spiritual world, so far as to have in it almost no sense whatever of any reality in things unseen and eternal."[4] According to Nevin, this limited perception of ours misses the "open communication" and "free intelligible correspondence" among all modes of being, "between the spiritual and natural worlds."[5] The evidence of our fallen perception appears "in the plain fact, that the two faculties of the will and the understanding no longer act . . . in quiet harmony."[6] Of course, said Nevin, it is our privilege to believe that open perception is "not wanting still in ten thousand other planets, peopled like ours with human life."[7]

CATHOLICITY NOW AND NOT YET

The will and the understanding of the individual are reunited in Christ, whose mystical union provides the nurture for the transformation of our own will and understanding. Thus is provided the true ground of ethics and the resource for dealing with the meaning of history. There is a radical catholicity at work in history, moving everything toward a more universal and open communication. It is radical because it must reject all partial claims to universality, while at the same time acknowledging the presence of universality in the call for greater realization that is latent in all achievement and aspiration.

Thus, the reality of catholicity is no vague dedication to universality, even in some morally ideal sense. Rather, it is the discovery of wholeness amid the penultimate claims of the world, as expressed in human experience. History is invested with the real presence of its universal meaning. In Christ, says Nevin, the order and constitution of nature were invested with a reality it could not realize by its own reason or its own labors. The course of history is altered; the presence of Christ is forever the warrant of existence. There has been a marriage, a union, that could not have taken place if "the constitution of the one had not been of *like sort* with that of the other, (man made in the image truly of God), so as to admit and require such union as the last and only perfect expression of the world's life."[8]

In 1845, in an essay for the *Weekly Messenger,* Nevin responded to the critics of his article on pseudo-Protestantism and his sermon "Catholic Unity." By the Incarnation, Nevin reminds his readers, "our nature as a whole was lifted from its fallen state, and brought into union with God."[9] Our nature is thus lifted to the form of a new creation in Christ, "not to continue in him as a separate individual; but to reveal itself progressively."[10] This progressive revelation works with radical force in the world, rejecting the exclusive and sectarian in favor of the more inclusive and catholic character of its continuing presence. "The old nature is not at once destroyed; but the new nature of Christ is inclosed in it."[11] As a son of the subtle exclusivity nurtured by the Church in its struggle to communicate the inclusivity of its truth, Nevin could not relinquish the right of "believers" to *claim* the "new creation." The Reformation had added special force to these claims of exclusivity, but they had already been present in the imperial pretensions of Roman Catholicism.

CATHOLICITY AND THE CHURCH

Nevin, like many theologians of his day, does not seem to recognize the radical catholicity of his own thought. He sought to make a distinction "between the person of Christ in an individual view and his person considered generically."[12] This distinction, he maintained, had not been made by Calvin or the Reformed tradition. Failure to understand this was usually a factor in attitudes toward the Eucharist because there was little recognition of the fact that the humanity of Christ was active in the world as a new creation. Consideration of the person of Christ in the individual view led people to assume that "he is not now present so far as his human form is concerned in the world. The constituent elements of his body pass not over in any sense to his people." Considered generically, however, the humanity of Christ "*is* present in the world, through all time, not in the power of his divine nature simply, but in the power also of his human nature."[13]

When Nevin contemplates the nature of that presence, he sees it as the life of the Church as extension or continuation of Christ's life. The question we must ask is whether "the life of the Church" is *confined* to the religious tradition long associated with the institutional state of Christianity. The nature of that institutional condition has been much different in the American context than in prior European history. As a matter of fact, it may well be the sectarian and utilitarian character of American Christianity that requires a different interpretation of Nevin's claims for "the life of the Church." What he called the "attenuated sensuousness" of our American spirituality constantly reduces the constitution of grace to "the order of mere nature."[14] The radical catholicity of Nevin's thought, on the other hand, suggests that the universality and wholeness of Christ's generic humanity are present in the world, celebrated by the Church, but not confined to the Church's celebration or to the penultimate formulation of dogmatic systems. Christ is present, but not captive, to Church or world. The issue, in Nevin's own mind, is whether "symbolical" books are capable of communicating the generic presence without limiting it to the individual understanding or experience, *separately or collectively* considered. This insight of Nevin's, set forth in the essay "Catholicism," is not always active in his own deliberations.

It seems that a certain utilitarianism asserts itself from time to time so that he confuses the "proper glory of the gospel" with the well-being of the "Christian religion." "The great problem of religion," he states in his article "The Mystical Union," "in the case of man, is to effect a reconciliation, and inward free union, between the divine nature and the human. This problem has never been satisfied by any system *lower* than Christianity."[15] Here he succumbs to a sectarian judgment about systems that leads him to say, for example, that "[e]ven Judaism here came short of the end, toward which all its institutions struggled."[16] Yet the generic humanity of Christ must already have been present in the Hebrew people, even though it may not have demonstrated the extent of atonement required to "effect a reconciliation, and inward free union, between the divine nature and human."

In the essay "Catholicism," Nevin provides a key to understanding the radical character of the catholicity of the generic humanity of Christ. The term "catholic," he reminds his readers, is generally understood to be of the same sense as "universal." Yet the problem encountered in the use of the latter term is that its meaning is commonly understood in a way that compromises "the true force of the term catholic." When we substitute the word "universal" for the word "catholic," out of some priggish anti-Romanist piety or rationalism, we tend, therefore, to lose a fundamental dimension of the attribute itself.

ALLNESS AND WHOLENESS

Generically speaking, universality is for most of us a reference to "allness." We think of "*all* the trees in a forest, *all* the stars, all human beings," says Nevin. Thus we may imagine something being universal if it embraces *all* the individual entries of a given factor. We compute in abstraction the actual number of single things and posit "a totality which exists only in the mind and is strictly dependent on the objects considered in their individual character."[17] According to this conception, Christianity is "catholic" if and when it "universally" embraces *all* the people in the world. Although this notion seems very concrete and factual, it is actually an abstraction because it is dependent on our ability to collect and classify individual existences by references to previously determined common properties. This would mean, according to Nevin, that the catholicity or universality referred to is "ever . . . a limited and finite generality." Catholicity remains in this sense an abstraction, unrealizable and unrecognizable because individual existences are always more than they seem to be. In other words, we imagine the universal only by way of projecting our limited sense of the individual. Our understanding of the catholic and universal is therefore based entirely on the constitution of nature itself. The universal is merely the imagined collectivity of individuals as we know, observe, and count them.

When Christians and churches act on this abstract notion of catholicity, they attempt some kind of mechanical unification of the human race.

> According to this view, the great purpose of the gospel is to save men from hell, and bring them to heaven; this is accomplished by the machinery of the atonement and justification by faith, carrying along with it a sort of

magical supernatural change of state and character by the power of the Holy Ghost, in conformity with the use of certain means for the purpose on the part of men; and so now it is taken to be the great work of the Church to carry forward the process of deliverance, almost exclusively under such mechanical aspect, by urging and helping as many souls as possible in their separate individual character to flee from the wrath to come and to secure for themselves through the grace of conversion a good hope against the day of judgment.[18]

However, when we remember that "pure naked individuality is an abstraction for which there is no place in the concrete human world," we are face-to-face with the knowledge that the idea of redemption implies of necessity far more than any deliverance that can take place in our lives separately considered.

The true force of the term "catholic" is more closely expressed in the word "whole" than in the word "all," wrote Nevin. Here the generality intended is not abstract but concrete. The generality is infinite yet realized. Wholeness is an organic unity, not a mechanical one. The parts of the whole draw their being from the universal. Wholeness is very present, very concrete, but points to a reality greater than the individual parts separately or collectively considered. For example, the *whole* person is not merely *all* the elements and powers that enter empirically into her constitution, but this living constitution is in fact more general than those elements and powers. What these latter are, in fact, is derived from the wholeness in which they live and move and have their being. The catholicity represented by Christ's kingdom is organic and concrete. It exists in the world in and through the many parts of which it is composed. "It must be regarded as going before them in the order of actual being, as underlying them at every point, and as comprehending them always in its more ample range."[19]

Nevin thought that the catholicity represented by the Kingdom of God permits no restriction with regard to geographical or national distinction. It may not be thought of as penetrating only one or another aspect of human experience. This means, of course, that it is not limited to the institutional life of Christianity or its religious system. However, this implication is bypassed by Nevin even though he acknowledges that nothing really human is beyond the scope of the Kingdom of God as embodied in the generic humanity of Christ. "The grand test of its truth is its absolute adequacy to cover the field of human existence at all points, its *catholicity* in the sense of measuring the entire length and breadth of man's nature. Either it is no redemption for humanity at all, or no constituent interest of humanity may be taken as extrinsical ever to its rightful domain."[20] As a matter of fact, argued Nevin, "no redemption can be real for man singly taken, or for any particular man, which is not at the same time for humanity . . . as a whole."[21]

For Nevin, Christianity is catholic because it shares eucharistically in the world as a whole. That is to say, the only response to the new creation in Christ is thankful participation in the bread and wine of this world as it has had its meaning revealed in the human life (Body and Blood) of Jesus Christ. "All stands," said Nevin, not on the interpretation of fragmentary texts of Scripture but "on the stand-point of the interpreter, and the comprehensive catholicity of his view."[22] The ultimate sense of this world as brought to awareness in personality is present in the continuing Incarnation of Jesus Christ; this power will not cease to work in the world until it embraces the whole of being. God has acted in this way. This is action for the wholeness of humanity; it is not possible that such action should be directed toward individuals in the hope that they, collectively considered, will make the truth universally valid. This would mean that the individual's judgment and conversion are greater than the redemption that has been accomplished. It would make the wholeness of the Kingdom of God dependent on the consummate action of individuals in nature. This would be no wholeness, no universality, at all—no redemption.

CATHOLICITY, MISSIONS, AND OTHER RELIGIONS

The implications of Nevin's radical catholicity are important for understanding the missionary task of Christianity and for its relationship to "other religions." They are significant also to a clarification of the relation of religion and the Republic, to a comprehension of the arts and literature, and to the social and economic order. We shall return to these issues later; however, here it may be necessary to point to their significance in relation to the understanding of Nevin's catholicity.

First, Nevin informs us that the proper catholicity or wholeness represented by Christianity "by no means implies the necessary salvation of *all* [people]." This is the error of universalists, who confound the idea of the *whole* with the notion of *all*. The world is redeemed intensively, although many individuals may never share in a saving recognition of that fact. There may be many people born into the natural order of the world (the posterity of Adam) who gain no insight into their natural inclinations or the partiality of their knowledge and experience. They may live and die without the appreciative awareness of their life in the generic humanity of Christ. This fact in no way diminishes the universality of Christ's life and work. Hundreds of blossoms may wither and fall from the tree, says Nevin, without in any way impairing the truth of the whole life of the tree as that is expressed in the fruit that appears and toward which that life tends from the beginning.

The fate, therefore, of those individuals whose lives are not enlightened by their awareness of "the whole life of the tree" does not die with their falling. For their own destiny is somehow part of the fruit that appears as a sign of the wholeness expressed by the tree. This does not mean that Christianity has no missionary responsibility. Mission and evangelism proceed on two levels: the Church must take its eucharistic life into the world, to permit individuals to accept the discipline and nurture essential to "enlightenment"— conversion, transformation, a salvational appropriation of redemption. The Church must also take up "the living economy of the world" into itself, or, more probably, "the power of Christianity should be wrought intensively into the whole of civilization." That, too, is a missionary task, in which the catholicity of the Church is an article of *faith* expressed in *all* ages; it is merely an expectation of what may become true *in the future*. The gospel must be taught to those who will listen and respond eucharistically to its presence. But it must also be celebrated as it shapes the orders of human existence themselves. This is mission far more near to the "redemption of the world, and of far more need at this time, for the bringing in of the millenium [*sic*], than the conversion of all India and China."[23] Thousands, as individuals, may fail to be born into this higher power of our universal nature, just as many thousands are not fully born into the natural power of being. This fact in no way confines the character of the power of itself.

Because the wholeness in question is not synonymous with allness, the quantitative individuality of nature, it is not subject to an abstract doctrine of election that selects a given number for the purpose of salvation. Redemption is not confinable. It is radical in its rejection of any final claim to the explanation or power of the individual, yet it is present in its wholeness at any time, any age.

Nevin's thought has creative implications for the relationship of Christianity to other religions. Here again, however, he is unable to accept those implications because Western history was not yet willing to release many thinkers from the imperialistic and exclusionary claims of culture and religion. Nevin informs his readers that the catholicity represented in Christ belongs to no single sphere of the natural order. "Even *religion,* which claims to be the last sense of man's life from the start, and which is therefore in consistency bound and urged under all forms to assert some sort of whole or universal title in its own favor, is found to be in truth unequal always to this high pretension, till it comes to its own proper and only sufficient completion in Christ."[24] This is a profound statement, yet still Nevin takes it to mean that the "proper and only sufficient completion in Christ" means Christianity *as a religion*. He compares the latter to "paganism," "Mohammedanism," and "Judaism," instead of comparing all religions (including Christianity) to the reality represented in and by Christ. His own radical catholic perspective implied that religion *"under all forms"* is under radical judgment—found "unequal to its high pretension" to universal title of the wholeness that is present in Christ. No religion has within it the power "to possess and represent in full harmony the *whole* idea of humanity." There is a contradiction in religionist claims to wholeness, a contradiction that becomes absurd when we ask ourselves whether the baptism of all the people of the world would signal the fullness of the Kingdom of God. The contradiction is not resolved *in the religion* of Christianity, as Nevin sometimes would have it; it is resolved in the catholicity of the Church as the body of Christ, a mystical body that claims nothing for itself but rises from the dead disorders of the world. "Only what is in this way *deeper than all* besides," says Nevin, "can be at the same time truly catholic, of one measure with the whole compass and contents of our universal life." [25]

Christianity's relationship to others is one of utter humility in this regard. Its status *as a religion* is as the status of any other. Its uniqueness is that it plays upon the consciousness of the mystical body of Christ, celebrating the present wholeness of that body in the world as of "one measure with the whole compass and contents of our universal life." This must mean that Christianity lives under the same radical judgment of its pretensions as any other religion. All religions must end, and perhaps know with T. S. Eliot that "In my beginning is my end. . . . [E]ach venture is a new beginning, a raid on the inarticulate with shabby equipment always deteriorating." [26] Religion itself dissolves; it is a constant and futile human invention that bears the force of its own undoing. Each religion is worth something of what it reveals, as Nevin puts it, of "the inmost fact of man's nature," a nature that is invaded by a new creation that reveals the partiality of its experience.

A CATHOLICITY OF CHURCH AND STATE

Nevin's radical catholicity also addresses the issue of the relationship of Church and state and thus provides insight into the American social and political order itself. He was aware of the growing dissociation of the two orders of human nature. Many Americans held it as a moral truism that the "total disruption of Church and State," their absolute separation, is the "only order that can at all deserve to be respected as rational." Yet such circumstances as those are false to the true idea of the gospel and demonstrate the loss of moral imagination in the actual state of the world.[27] Under its natural and secular aspects, human beings own a proper measure of freedom. Freedom is that quality of our being that directs us toward the loving and self-giving God whose wholeness is present in our natural existence, as evidenced by Christ and the Church. The state exists in the natural order to guarantee that freedom. The Church exists, on the other hand, to remind the state that it is not the possessor or the authoritarian enforcer of that freedom. What the state exists to protect is ultimately to be realized by the catholicity represented by the Church. In the eschaton, the end beyond history, the state is swallowed up by the Church—the constitution of grace fulfills and glorifies what the constitution of nature aspires to and dimly recognizes. The ideal relationship in nature is that Church and state be bound "into one with free inward reconciliation."[28]

Nevin took issue with Richard Rothe of Heidelberg University, who in his *Origins of the Christian Church* and *Theological Ethics* had arrived at the conclusion that the Church is destined to be absorbed by the state. Rothe had taken the position, according to Nevin, that the state is the basic moral organism of existence. Therefore, the ultimate goal of the state is to fulfill all that is part of moral aspiration, including the sense of religion.[29] The true sense of the Reformation is evident here because it represented a rejection of "old Catholic doctrine of the Church." The Reformation made room for a new and instrumental notion of the Church as that organization which is necessary to infuse the state with the moral insight and conscience essential to its own consummation. In this view of Rothe's, said Nevin, the Church eventually fulfills its responsibility and passes away. The problem, however, is that the Church will not want to give up easily and will try to assert its right to continue to be the agent of religion and morality. Conflict, oppression, and restraint will be the order of the day. The Church will try to reject the state as representative of "the true order of religion."

Rothe's error, in Nevin's thinking, was his assumption "that the economy of the world, naturally considered, must be regarded as carrying in itself all the necessary elements and conditions of a perfect humanity."[30] This assumption would seem justifiable if the natural order is apprehended as self-redemptive, wholly independent—if our ordinary perception is adequate to the resolution of the historical process. From this point of view it would seem proper that the goals of natural existence should not be unrealized. If it is the decision of humankind that it wishes to achieve its own ideal end—the realization of a utopian dream, let us say, and if it is entirely within the power of the human enterprise to bring about its intentions, then, of course, the Church shall pass away as soon as it has sufficiently motivated the state to its own natural purposes.

However, from the perspective of the Church as the mystical Body of Christ, redemption "is more than the carrying out of the natural order of the world to any merely natural end."[31] The "kingdom of heaven" is an order of being that is more than the system of natural ideas and practices that dominates the natural order. In Christ the natural order has been invested with the "constitution of grace" that will eventually fulfill the expectations of human history in a manner quite beyond the capacities of nature and history as we know them. "The Church will not lose itself in the state; but it will be the state rather that shall be found then to have vanished away in the Church."[32] *In history* the Church always continues as the manifestation of that which transcends nature, else it is nothing at all. Protestantism is not identical, says Nevin, with the primitive Christianity of the postapostolic community, which itself developed into Roman Catholicism. Protestantism is instead the most recent development of Christianity *out of* Roman Catholicism. It is therefore evidence of the principle of catholicity at work and a "supernatural fact" for its time. What Protestantism shall develop into—what it shall become—remains to be seen; but it *shall be,* according to Nevin. It is the mission of the Church to guide the state into the new creation.

A CATHOLICITY OF CULTURE

It is rather obvious, from all I have shown of Nevin's thought in this chapter, that the social and cultural order in all its forms is under the same mandate as the state. Art, literature, philosophy, economics, and social life are the field of labor for the Church. Human beings exist only in groups and societies. The idea of the single individual is an abstraction, for we are what we are always, only in virtue of those others who are set in apposition to us. The entire world must be appropriated into the new creation. Wherever human life is, there must the Church be also. Our lives have no character whatever aside from the things we express as art, music, literature. They have no existence except in relation to families, groups, states, and in pursuit of food and shelter. Therefore, it is absurd to address the Christian gospel to the abstract individual alone. Rather, it must be addressed to the orders of thought and action that are the contextual expression of our humanity. This does not mean that individuals are not addressed at all. In a sense, the dialectic of the inward and outward, the intensive and extensive, is always present in Nevin's thinking. The *wholeness* of the Church may not be identical with the numerical *all* of the natural and collective order of humankind, but the evangelization of the world "*in extenso* . . . is generally admitted."[33] The catholicity represented by the gospel is for the world, not merely for a section of humanity, particular nations or races. Its power of liberation and redemption must be carried "to every creature," because all creatures share the inheritance of Christ's mystical presence. Yet Nevin's emphasis is on the intensive rather than the extensive. Extending the gospel to *all* has ultimate significance only to the degree that the *interior* life, as represented in human thought and activity, is possessed by Christ. "The work of the gospel is too generally thought of as something comparatively outward [extensive] to the life of [humankind], and so a power exerted on it mechanically from abroad for its salvation, rather than a real redemption brought to pass in it from the inmost depths of its own nature."[34]

It is not possible, according to Nevin, for "the proper reality as exhibited in the Incarnate Word" to be grasped merely by the natural understanding of either one person or many. Nor is it to be known as a sort of abstract deism, in which the idea of God is held steadily as something outside of the world, a power working from beyond and occasionally breaking in upon the settled order of things. It is not a reality that is magical or apparitional—some pre-conceived notion of a Messiah who will be "a sign from heaven, some out-ward supernatural demonstration." This reality is present in the flesh, in hu-manity—in the fallen natural constitution of the world, but in a new creation that can only be apprehended when we have faced the fragmentation, the partiality, of our ordinary comprehension. Natural understanding makes for a confusion of claims, a kind of sectarianism of the mind and spirit. The result is a continuing sense of frustration—not yet convincing *everyone* (all) of the validity or our ideas and experiences. This is characteristic of life in the old creation, but the new creation exhibits no such fractionality and imperfection. It is wholeness itself, shared in the midst of imperfect existence. "The univer-sal gospel lay hid in his person from the very beginning," said Nevin in a *Concio Ad Clerum* delivered in Grace Church, Pittsburgh, on November 18, 1863, at the opening of the first General Synod of the German Reformed Church in America. "All its privileges and powers, and its opportunities and resources of salvation, all its doctrines and all its precepts, were comprised in the constitution of his theanthropic life."[35]

BEYOND JUSTIFICATION BY FAITH

The Incarnation is something very human, but it is the beginning of our understanding of what is human. It draws after it, and in the way of certain historical development, the whole work of redemption within all creations of the human spirit—its imaginings, aspirations, and struggles. The truth and reality of this wholeness can only be known on its own terms—"not on the strength of any evidence from a sphere lower than itself, but through an act of submission in the first place to what it claimed to be as a new order of life altogether in its own sphere."[36] This is what has been called "faith" by the Church; however, it is not a mere "act of submission" in the Tertullian sense of the affirmation of the absurd but rather a trusting in the right disposition of the mind. The ordinary mind may incline itself in preparation for the truth of the Incarnation, but it cannot be sufficient to authenticate the actual sense of the mystical union of God and humankind. That union is a catholic wholeness quite beyond the ability of the natural understanding to take measure of it. It is a reality that draws us into its vision in order that we may understand the ultimate order and meaning of existence, a reality that stands in radical judgment on claims to comprehend it in fullness. Faith, then, is the proper response to the radical catholicity of the reality historically embodied in Christ. Faith is "the organ or faculty in us, by which through divine grace we yield ourselves, at once passively and actively, to the authority of the Gospel, regarded as a true revelation of God's presence in the world, and so make room for it to accomplish its saving work upon us in its own way."[37] Faith thus becomes an epistemological principle tied to the catholic reality of "God's presence in the world."

The fact of faith as a mode of knowing the wholeness of reality means that Christian thought, considered as theoretical or practical, must in the nature of the case be Christological. This is not some patronizing or imperious assumption about Christianity as a religion, but represents the living and historical fact of a new creation that is *more than* the ability of representatives of the old creation to comprehend. It can only be appropriated by faith as it assists the understanding in awareness of what is more than its natural apprehension. Nevertheless, Nevin is concerned to keep faith from becoming an abstraction or a Gnostic palliative. He wants his readers and auditors to understand that the fact of the revelation of the new creation is historical, not to be torn from the organic existence of this divine constitution. "Regeneration holds a supernatural mystery in Christ only."[38] Presumably this requires faithfulness to the Body of Christ which exists by the sustenance of his mystical presence.[39]

For Nevin the Reformation doctrine of justification by faith is always in danger of becoming justification by fancy, feeling, or resignation. It may represent a failure of the dialectic of inward and outward, inasmuch as it may appear to be satisfied with the presence of an ideal, an expectation, in the mind of the individual, separately taken. But the Church is conceived "as a real outward as well as inward constitution, having in such view of its own organism as a single whole, and keeping up a true identity with itself in space and time." [40] The Church must always embody the mystery it represents. True mystery is the evidence of a new creation in the midst of the old, and requires the dialectic, therefore, of outward manifestation and inward realization. Justification makes sense only in the mystery of the Church's wholeness, a catholicity objectively invested in the partial climate of the fallen world. The catholic truth of the gospel does not exist in negotiation with the private judgment of humankind; it exists in and for the world as an objective reality represented by Christ.

As Glenn Hewitt has assessed it, "Faith is not the principle of this life, but the means on the human side by which it enters the person." [41] Faith is actually the refinement of what has entered our lives by the Holy Spirit at the sacramental moment of baptism. Baptism is "by water and the Spirit"—"the introduction of a new divine principle into the being of the soul . . . not in any way of nature, or from the powers of man's life existing before itself. As related to all this it is transcendental and supernatural. It is in such view the opposite of all earthly natural birth, a birth literally and strictly *from above*." [42] Only "from above" is wholeness possible; only "from above" can that wholeness enter the world to take possession of it inwardly and outwardly, intensively and extensively. We may *together* believe in "the Holy Catholic Church," not separately as either individuals or sects. No mere sect or fragment of the Church may responsibly appropriate the title "Catholic" for itself. By the same token, no mere humanistic or humanitarian ideology or program may equate itself with the Kingdom of God or consider itself universal. Such "secular" notions are "of one measure with the natural life of man, because [they add] nothing to this and [have] no power whatever to lift it into any higher sphere." [43]

The radical catholicity in Nevin's thought may have been too much for his own religiosity in its time, but it was a profound and liberating concept. It challenged the presumptions of Protestantism, Roman Catholicism, and Anglicanism. It reminded the conversionist mentality of American revivalism that its view of the universal was excessively utilitarian and privatistic—relying on the sense of catholicity as allness. Roman Catholicism tended to rely on a rationalistic supernaturalism that did not adequately reside in the natural order. Anglicanism made absurd claims about the ideal of episcopacy and of a pre–Roman Catholic Church that denied the principle of historical development and led to formalistic sectarianism.

Nevin's radical catholicity embodied a dialectic of a realized wholeness and a radical prophetic challenge to ideological or practical claims upon that wholeness. Radical catholicity maintained a dialectic of intensive and extensive realization, a dialectic that was to extend the meaning of the Incarnation of

Christ into all orders of society and culture, even as it sought to offer the people invitation into communion with the mystical presence of Christ in the world. For Nevin ecclesiology and Christology were inseparable; so after all, is the theology of culture not to be divorced from ecclesiology and Christianity. This principle is very evident in the public theology of John Nevin.

five

TOWARD A THEOLOGY
OF HISTORY

A people without history is like wind on the buffalo grass.
—Teton Lakota Proverb

On the subject of history, John Nevin had this to say:

> The rationality of history is a postulate of our reason and of our religious
> reason in particular. . . . [I]t has not been proved that we are capable of
> determining the life of the world by simply studying the life of man. . . .
> It has been supposed that [the] key is to be found in the political and scien-
> tific life of man, but it has proved to be unsatisfactory; and we are therefore
> compelled to admit that man's chief end lies beyond *the* present life and order
> of things.[1]

Nevin's conviction of the importance of history was not always as keen as it
was to become in the Mercersburg years and during his latter years as a professor at Franklin and Marshall College in Lancaster. "As I had studied it at
Princeton," he wrote of church history in 1870, "it was for me the poorest
sort of sacred science. There was in truth no science in it; and its associations
could hardly be called sacred, as they certainly were not edifying in any way."[2]
He was later to discover something living where formerly he had observed
only a dead and dreary past, a "valley of dry bones." Although he referred
specifically to *church* history, he awakened to an understanding of history itself,
an understanding that influenced his religious thought and established a theology of history as the foundation of his theoretical enterprise. His reading of
German scholars such as Neander and his association with Philip Schaff were
to complement his growing uneasiness with the mechanical approach to history that was dominant in America, especially in its theological schools. Ideas
especially were assumed to be fixed and insular notions that moved through
time unaffected by change. Suffice it to say that much history is still taught in

this manner, as reflected in the apathy of students toward the dry bones of historical data.

When Nevin inherited the chair of church history at Western Theological Seminary in 1837, he was provided with the opportunity to begin the development of his historical perspective. At first he stuck with the established approach to history as exemplified in the work of the German historian Johannes Lorenz von Mosheim. However, he avoided the question of whether history had any meaning other than as a record of the ongoing process of events. The question of meaning is always a difficult subject for the academic mind to handle, and Nevin found it no less difficult in spite of his growing sense of development and context. At Princeton Samuel Miller had supplemented the mechanical history of Mosheim by suggesting that his students "read 'the pietistically feeble' English historian Joseph Milner."[3] All this added up to was a pietistic review of the dead, outward facts of doctrine. At first Nevin did not "feel at liberty to attempt any material innovation on the course of instruction as it had stood before," but the effects of Neander's idea of history "broke up [his] dogmatic slumbers" like an "awakening of the soul."[4]

DISCOVERING HISTORY

The development of his theology of history was under way; it was becoming an objective movement determined by forces at work within it toward a meaningful end. "There is a divinity even in profane history," he explained in mature reflection on the course of his thought, a divinity "which shapes it everywhere to the service of a divine universal plan," a plan revealed in "the history of God's Holy Catholic Church."[5] This insight is essential to the maintenance of a "true liberal culture. . . . There can be no right knowledge of the world, and no right standing or working in the world without it."[6]

The Teton Lakota proverb at the beginning of this chapter reminds us that "a people without history is like wind on the buffalo grass." Presumably no people can actually exist without a history, inasmuch as history refers to that story that links us together with our grandfathers and grandmothers. However, Americans in the nineteenth century had recently severed links with the political story of Great Britain and were engaged in a contemplation of modern society that seemed to derive its manners, morals, and metaphysics from the vast new continent itself. This contemplation had begun even before the period of colonization; it had begun with the vision of a "land promised to the saints," a vision that detached the imagination of transplanted Europeans from the Old World of their grandfathers and grandmothers.

In a sense the Euro-Americans were not unlike many of the Native Americans who had preceded them as residents of the American wilderness. As Frederick Turner tells it in *Beyond Geography,* when "the Lakota and Cheyenne tribes reverted from a semi-sedentary existence to the life of hunters on the Great Plains . . . they loved the new life so much that farming and a settled existence came to seem repugnant and restrictive to them [in] their new habitat . . . a grassland dark with huge herds of bison, deer, and antelope."[7] The wilderness and the bold new society seemed to obliterate history, to return the people to the marvels of Eden or to the land of plenty promised in the time of the ancestors. J. Hector St. John Crèvecoeur wrote of the "licentious idle life" of the hunter, a life that leads to "fatal degradation" when it is united with want and bad luck. The "sweet accents" of religion itself are "lost in the immensity of these words," wrote Crèvecoeur in his *Letters from an American Farmer* (1782). "Men thus placed are not fit either to receive or remember its mild instructions; they want temples and ministers, but *as soon as men cease to remain at home,* and begin to lead an erratic life, *let them be either tawny or white,* they cease to be its disciples."[8]

Crèvecoeur may have been a bit extravagant in his claims and somewhat distorted in his understanding of the natives. However, he reminds us that Europeans and "Indians" may both become "like wind on the buffalo grass." History for natives was the communication with those who have peopled the world before the present time. History for the natives was a story without time that helped the people overcome vertigo when the wind was strong on the buffalo grass. History for the Euro-American was the memory of frustration, obligation, and oppression that lingered like heavy fog over wagons tilting westward. They were people on the march, with no attachment to the land, removed from nature and revering the promised land only as an image in the destiny they shared in covenant with a god outside nature. Europeans were peoples who had ceased to "remain at home"; their contemplation of the lush new continent was more a contemplation of promise than of the land itself or its indigenous inhabitants. Unlike the Lakota, the Euro-Americans held little attachment to either the soil or the bison and antelope.

BEYOND MILLENNIAL ILLUSION

America meant promise; it meant deliverance from the past. Its religious life had quickly adapted itself to the symbolism of promise and sought to escape from history. The Evangelical message of salvation that was being shaped as a new religion out of the crisis of the deteriorating Old World was essentially an escape from history. For some it was fashioned out of disillusionment created by the loneliness, frustration, famine, and disease experienced in a land that did not seem to conform to its "promise." But for others, like Lyman Beecher and Charles Grandison Finney (though they were not in agreement in all matters), the gospel directed toward the salvation of individual souls would fashion moral energies essential to ward off ignorance, vice, and superstition in the making of the West. Yet even in the struggle to create institutions suitable to the new civilization in the making, there was the assumption that to give allegiance to the past was to be victimized by feudal ignorance and servitude. America's attention to land and institution was a dedication to promise, a dedication that created its own insular "history," which, in effect, is not history at all. Even though Ralph Waldo Emerson learned much from the past, he saw the redemption of the soul as the preparation for life in paradise and understood the wisdom of Homer, Pindar, and Socrates as evidence of a principle of immediate relationship to nature. "In the woods is perpetual youth" because there "we return to reason and faith" so that the "currents of the Universal Being circulate" through us.[9] The woods were the cradle of "promise" for the salvation of the individual—his escape from history. In the midst of a people without history, Emerson could still say:

> Our age is retrospective. It builds the sepulchres of the fathers. It writes biographies, histories and criticism. The foregoing generation beheld God and nature face to face; we, through their eyes. Why should not we also enjoy an original relation to the universe?[10]

John Nevin was an American theologian who discovered history among a people who sought to escape it. By the time he arrived at Mercersburg in 1840, he was ready to apply his sense of history to a series of theological and public issues. Sectarianism, reflected in what he called the American "sect system," is merely a history-less Christianity, he wrote. The many sects that sacralized the American landscape were but rampant attempts to "enjoy an original relation to the universe." The countryside was decorated with simple meetinghouses that resounded with plaintive cries and songs that pitched and quaked between the somber valley of death and the joyous vaults of heaven. Conversion became the ecstatic enjoyment of original and private relation, an ascension from the relentless course of history, private and social.

However, conversion in the historical sense is a complementation, as it is in the game of football, where the "extra point" is a conversion that completes and supplements what has been done before. In effect, history is inescapable; no conversion ever transcends the past absolutely. A conversion is a religious complementation of the religious pattern that preceded. In an essay on philosophy Nevin wrote:

> History implies organic unity and progress. It is just the opposite of chaos. Such onward movement, exhibiting the present always as at once the birth of the past and the womb of the future, belongs to the very conception of humanity. . . . Distribution in time, and distribution in space, are alike necessary, to represent the one vast, magnificent fact, through which the idea of man is made real. To be human, then, is to be at the same time historical. . . .[11]

Conversion itself, therefore, although often characterized by private personal manifestation, is really always *inter*personal and historical—exhibiting the traits of unity and development. Americans would have a difficult time understanding or accepting such notions as these. They frequently thought of themselves as Darwinian "sports," able to enjoy Emerson's original and direct relation to the universe. Their religious behavior was becoming very much dedicated to Phrygian dance, said Nevin, being interpreted as a revival of religion. Real revival occurs as intensity, discernment, and renewed responsibility overtake us in the course of the nurturing, ongoing life of the Church.[12] However, this understanding of the organic nature of the historical Church was too much for the pragmatic "new Americans" to contemplate. Even Lutherans found Nevin's theology to be "an effort to revive the errors of bygone ages, from which it was fondly hoped our American Churches had finally and forever escaped."[13] He was accused of "semi-Romanism," of fostering a revival of exploded superstitions.[14]

BEYOND HISTORY-LESS SECTARIANISM

By the time of the writing of the essays entitled "The Sect System" in 1849, published in the first volume of the *Mercersburg Review*, John Nevin had established the relevance of history as essential to self-understanding, theological wisdom, and American destiny. His understanding of history was an antidote to an emergent nationalism, a subject I shall discuss in the next chapter. The occasion for his often caustic attack on the irrationality of reigning modern sects was the appearance of John Winebrenner's revision and republication of I. D. Rupp's *History of All the Religious Denominations in the United States.* Winebrenner was an expatriate of the German Reformed Church, having been convinced by "Methodistical" and revivalist piety to found his own true church. Nevin had already castigated "Winebrennerians" as engaging in "the sport of quacks" in his 1843 work *The Anxious Bench.*[15] They were sectarians who like to "feel faith," a reduction of religion that needed no history, only the enjoyment of an original and immediate beholding of God face-to-face. "A Winebrennerian camp meeting," wrote Nevin, "surrendering itself to the full sway of this spirit [the delusion of confusing this 'feeling' with the true peace of religion], will carry with it a more disastrous operation than the simple Anxious Bench in a respectable and orderly church." [16]

In his book Winebrenner was now engaging in sectarian history itself, said Nevin. The Rupp book had operated under the premise that one could avoid accusations of bias and unfair treatment by compiling a work in which each denomination would be "permitted to paint itself according to its own liking." [17] Such a work as this would be entirely free from faults of misrepresentation. "The idea of a history," said Nevin in criticism of this popular project, "requires it to be as much as possible objective, and independent of all personal reference and interests; whereas, in this case, full rein was given to the principle of subjectivity." [18] The project was a worthless literary salmagundi that did violence to the nature of history itself. Absolute objectivity is not possible, of course, but the subjectivity of history is always in obedience to the need to do justice to a vast network of outward observations, events, and ideas.

Nevin could not have understood the history of religions as an honest attempt to comprehend the system and Weltanschauung of those of another tradition, another "way." As we have seen, he was ultimately an apologist for "the Christian religion," even though he understood religion to be in a state of historical development and of judgment by the authority of the Kingdom of God. Yet he had claimed the modernist presuppositions of history as objective—something extended, "out there," to be *looked at*. History as object is not the same as "thing," person, or creature as object. The objectivity of history is a perspective of interpretation, of hermeneutical testing, that is akin to Nevin's idea of catholicity as wholeness. It is an awareness that subjectivity is of all modes of explanations most apropos only of the need to tell someone *how we feel*. History is a reminder that we live in a whole that is greater than the sum of its parts, more than our present analysis or vision of evidence can be trusted to provide.

In the study of religion we can never rely on subjective treatises. History is a recognition of the conditional character of the substance of religion and its method of interpretation. As explained in chapter 1, Nevin returned to an even more formal concern for history in his later years. One of his students, S. S. Kohler, took extensive notes on Nevin's "Philosophy of History" lectures at Franklin and Marshall College during the early 1870s, a few years before Nevin's final retirement. His notes record Nevin's thoughts about history as movement:

> This definition, however, is insufficient in itself. No definition in the start of a science ever amounts to much; for the terms that we use may call for new definitions. No definition ever makes a science intelligible. We can never understand what the definition means before we understand the science.[19]

Any effort to define history is especially dependent on the "science" itself, an enterprise of analysis and articulation of the wholeness of human circumstance. Even Rupp was disturbed by Winebrenner's usurpation of the former's "History." Winebrenner extended the catalog of "sects" from "between forty and fifty" to "upwards of seventy religious denominations." Apparently Rupp had not expected to produce "a true and complete history of sects," only an approximation that would assist the unprejudiced reader in drawing his own conclusions. Nevin understood Rupp's original intention but concluded that it confirmed the worthlessness of such a project when it was "viewed as a veritable History of Religious Denominations."[20] However, with Winebrenner's additions, the true nature of the book emerged. Winebrenner had compiled the revised work partly to demonstrate the truth and power of his own sectarian pretensions as founder of the General Eldership of the Church of God in North America.

With this insight carefully allied to his service, Nevin delivered a rather skillful backhand. Obviously, said Nevin, we misjudged this book. It deserves a more favorable response. Just because it is no "veritable and proper history" does not mean it is not an important book. "It is, in its own way, a most interesting and valuable Commentary on the Sect System," which any historian might read with great delight. The work certainly does "credit to the mind from which it sprang." A serious and thoughtful mind can reflect on this exhibit as it would on the contents of "Catlin's Indian Museum."[21] We are overwhelmed by the individually and separately considered entries in the gallery of portraits, and we recognize, said Nevin, that we shall be able to gaze upon these sectarian fancies "with curious admiration hereafter, when the sects themselves, in most cases (it is to be trusted) shall have passed away, with the Pottawottamies, into mere memory and song."[22]

The history-less character of the sectarian mind is vividly portrayed in the manner in which all sectarians agree in proclaiming the Bible the only guide of their faith. The history-less mind, be it Emerson's or Alexander Campbell's, fixes its gaze upon a principle of authority that aims to be clear of all dogma and opinion. With the Christian sects, of course, the twin principles of Bible and private judgment carry the day. It should be no difficult consideration to observe that sectarianism is not concerned with the wholeness and unity that history represents but with a collective gathering of "all" into a pattern of conformity. Bible and private judgment represent *failure* of authority; they lead to proliferation, not integrity. No sect in reality abides by the principles it asserts. Each "has a scheme of notions already at hand, a certain system of opinion and practice, which is made to underlie all this boasted freedom in the use of the Bible, leading private judgment along by the nose, and forcing the divine text always to speak in its own way." [23] This is because the history-less mind has nothing to contemplate but the outward notions and abstractions that are necessary to its own triumph.

The Bible is made into something it never was or was meant to be. It becomes an outward manifestation of authority in service to private judgment, a relic of truth and immediately accessible to the individual quest and its mandate to manipulate "all" others to its aims. "The idea of a living revelation *in the Bible*," wrote Nevin, "which must authenticate *it* [the Bible] and unfold its true sense, is but dimly, if at all, perceived." [24] The sect consciousness has no sense of historical continuity in the life of the Church; the system is entirely unhistorical, "protests against all previous history, except so far as it may seem to agree with what is thus found to agree with what is thus found to be true; in which case . . . the only real measure of truth is taken to be, not this *authority of history* at all, but the mind, simply, of the particular sect itself." [25]

THE UNHISTORICAL LEAPS OF PROTESTANT THOUGHT

Nevin's book-length essay "Early Christianity" was written in response to travel commentaries by two priests of the Church of England. Their reflections dealt mostly with the Roman Church as observed in Lyons and Milan. The commentaries were essentially Protestant, anti-Roman, and filled with the kinds of generalizations that Nevin found so objectionable in some Anglican attempts to justify the validity of their own church order by an unhistorical leap over the fourth to sixteenth centuries. Nevin was amused by the inability of the Anglican writers to explain the emergence of "truly evangelical faith" in Catholic writers like Charles Borromeo, Anselm, and Bernard. According to the Anglicans, these latter could only be understood as spiritual curiosities, grand exceptions to the history as commonly understood.

What seemed to Nevin an absurd mode of thinking led him into a careful study of the early Church and the movement of history. It is a blind prejudice, he wrote, "to suppose that the piety of the Roman Church . . . springs not from the proper life of the system itself, but is there rather by accident." [26] Modern religious thought relies heavily on the ill-conceived notion that certain ideas and practices of the past are nothing but superstitions and abuses that have been eliminated by the rationalism of the post-Enlightenment mind. There is the tendency to an unhistorical assumption that behind the corruptions of Roman Catholicism there existed a golden age of relatively pure religious faith that truly represented "the simplicity and spirituality of the proper divine model of the Church."[27] However, the historical mind thinks from a perspective of wholeness that recognized that the differences between earliest times and those that followed are to be understood as the onward course of things—a movement that from the very start was *toward* the order that afterward prevailed.[28]

The sectarian spirit may reside in many forms, said Nevin. Whether Anglican or Congregationalist, it ignores historical development. It thinks it is possible to repristinate what was present to the fourth, third, or second century. It ignores the fact that the past is only accessible in relation to that which emerged out of it and lives in the present moment. There is sectarian pretense in Protestantism and Romanism, according to Nevin, when their representatives refuse to acknowledge that God has entered history—the Incarnation *continues* to make a difference. There is the "necessity of a transition on the part of the Church through various stages of form . . . for the very purpose of bringing out more . . . fully always the true inward sense of its life."[29]

THE CATHOLICITY OF HISTORY

It should be evident that Nevin's discovery of the significance of history was accompanied by the image of catholicity. If the sectarian character of American Christianity was linked to the history-less inclination of the American mind, whether transcendentalist or Evangelical, it was also true that history reveals a catholicity, a wholeness, that rejects partial claims to that wholeness.

Nevin discovered this history-less claim to be very apparent in Anglicanism. He had followed the development of the Oxford movement in England. The early work of John Henry Newman, John Keble, and Edward Pusey had not gone unnoticed; indeed, Oxford and Mercersburg were concurrent movements on different sides of the Atlantic with similar, though hardly identical, agendas. Nevin wrote "The Anglican Crisis" in the same year (1851) he began to explore the nature of early Christianity. The Anglicans were responding to the political circumstances of their own land by trying to discover a principle of continuity with early Christianity that would vindicate the uniqueness of the Church of England. There were those who concluded that that principle was episcopacy, "handed down by outward succession, as a sort of primary divinely appointed mark and seal of the true Church."[30] It is on this principle, said Nevin, that "Anglicanism piques itself on being a *jure divino* succession of the old English branch of the Church Catholic, while for want of such accidents other Protestant bodies . . . have no right to put in any similar claim."[31] This glorification of the episcopate is historically unsound, continued Nevin. Fathers such as Cyprian, Ambrose, or Augustine may have valued episcopacy, but only as it lived in the eucharistic unity of the Church. The episcopacy of the first four or five centuries existed in harmony with elements that bore great resemblance to the later tradition of the Roman Church—elements which Anglicanism sought to establish as anti-Christian and false. The ecclesiastical troubles of England were, indeed, "eminently historical," according to Nevin; but their significance was not to be measured in the history-less claims of certain spokespersons for Anglicanism and its fixation on episcopacy as pristine Christianity.[32]

The importance of the Oxford Movement and the great church agitation in England was to be found in the realization that the course of religion is moving toward a new stage of development. What he described in "The Anglican Crisis" was in fact a Christian crisis according to Nevin. The course of Protestantism had been one of inward preparation for the moment when it could claim its own past, the Catholic substance it had lost in unthinking reaction against Roman Catholicism. The crisis in England was evidence of the activity of Incarnation in history; no phase of the Church's history may think of itself as consummate, arrested, completed. Protestantism is not a thing in itself but an emergence out of Roman Catholicism. Its failure to understand that had begun to stultify its development. The Tractarians in England were forcing the Church to come to terms with the course of history, which meant acknowledging the legitimacy of its past and being open to its future. The wholeness present in the catholicity of the Church constantly challenges it to accept the penultimate character of its knowledge and experience. This wholeness makes history the staging of the continuing struggle of inwardness and outwardness, the result of which is a new realization of catholicity. Inwardness cannot exist meaningfully by itself. "There must have been . . . a mighty disposition in the English mind towards Catholicism, or at least mighty dissatisfaction inwardly with Puritanism."[33] In America the chaos of the sect system and the inward egoism of revivalistic Evangelicalism were evidence of the need for coming to terms with the continuing outward manifestation of the Church as the Body of Christ in history. History is not meaningless, and "[t]he English movement falls in with this wide spread and *manifestly providential* tendency [that] shows again its vast historical significance and force."[34]

There was a tendency in the Oxford Movement to err in the direction of a mere *outward* claim to proper and original catholic order as represented in episcopacy. These pretensions rest on a very mechanical view of the Church, a kind of *jure divino* constitution in an outward style that presumes to uphold the faith and mystery of the one, holy, catholic, and apostolic Church.

> Faith in the Church, in the old ecclesiastical sense, is not a stiff persuasion merely that certain arrangements are of divine appointment, and a disposition to stickle for them accordingly as the lines and stakes that go to fix the conception; it is the apprehension rather of the Church as a living supernatural fact, back of all such arrangements, having its ground and force in the mystery of the Incarnation, according to the order of the ancient creed, and communicating to the marks and signs by which it is made visible every particle of virtue that is in them for any such end.[35]

Such an idea as this is historical; Nevin could not have made the observation without the dynamic view of history he had discovered in scholars like Neander. Nevin took very seriously the gospel promise "Lo I am with you always, even to the end of the world." That promise was substantial; it was not merely an assurance of subjective potential but an indication of the actual presence of a living constitution of grace, "a higher order of history."[36] The address of the gospel—"Lo I am with you"—was not to the private judgment of the sectarian mind but to the *world* through those who had been made one by the life and work of Christ. The world was on a different course, its history affected by a new creation, a constitution of grace. When, in the New Testament, human beings are aware of who Christ is, they are spoken of as being *in Christ,* says Nevin. "One or two instances of such language might bear, possibly, to be resolved into a strong figure of speech; although we should feel it a strange hyperbole, indeed, to speak even twice or once of the patriots of the American Revolution, as being *in George Washington.*"[37] In Christ the world is centered, drawn toward wholeness.

HISTORY AND INCARNATION

There were interpretations of the Incarnation such as those made by a writer in the *New York Observer* of September 8, 1848, who gave critical notice to an article by Philip Schaff. The critic did not understand Schaff because the latter's ideas savored of the transcendental, especially when Schaff affirmed that "the Lord is perpetually born anew in the hearts of believers." The critic's comments implied that the Incarnation "did not enter the organization of the world at all, as a fact of permanent force," wrote Nevin. "Probably he has no sense whatever of this organization, as a *vast whole completing* itself in man, and thus *reaching forward as a single historical process* from the beginning of the world to its end."[38] Such notions as the reviewer's plainly reveal the unhistorical mind of much of the American Evangelical and rationalist culture.

That mind does not recognize the world as organism or history, according to Nevin. The world is a vast sand heap in which individuals are thrown together outwardly as a kind of collectivity, "to be formed for eternity as so many separate units, each perfect and complete by itself." In this understanding the Incarnation is one of those naked units, as though the man Jesus is somehow mysteriously *made God* for himself alone, to whom we may then defer as to some idol or god of our choosing. Such a figure as this is an abstraction, said Nevin, inasmuch as separate existence is always conditioned universally by a general human substance beyond it. The only thing such a savior as this can effect is to provide the model and machinery of a functional atonement that carries with it "a sort of magical supernatural change of state and character . . . in conformity with the use of certain means for the purpose." The Church, then, becomes a functional association of those who know the magical and mechanical means and whose purpose it is to carry forward this work by urging and helping as many separate individuals as possible to flee the wrath of judgment and secure an entry into heaven through an experience of contrived conversion. The Church, therefore, is charged with collecting those separate individuals into an abstract *all* that marks the end of the Church's mission.[39]

However, this understanding of the Incarnation is unhistorical, uncatholic, and in conflict with the witness of church history and the New Testament. For Nevin, the Incarnation has an intensive effect on the life of the world; it has to do not with a merely extensive salvation, a deliverance in the form of outward power and function in the collection of individuals separately considered. The Christian gospel offers no mere theophany or avatar, "fantastically paraded . . . before men's eyes, only to be translated afterwards to heaven."[40] It elevates our general life, often in spite of or in transformation of our violence, greed, and continuing sinful behavior as individuals or churches. "History is made to possess contents by it, which had no place in it before."[41]

In *The Principle of Protestantism* (1845) Philip Schaff had espoused a theology of history that envisioned the end of all human divisions, all denominations and sects. Schaff's was an eschatological perspective that understood all realms of culture moving toward reconciliation and oneness. "One Spirit and one body! One Shepherd and one flock!"[42] The Church was the element, the force of meaning in the direction of history! The Church's own history moved through stages from Petrine legalism and authority to Pauline grace and freedom, to a synthesis in Johannine love of freedom in law. A grand reconciliation of culture and the Kingdom of God was in the making.[43]

John Nevin endorsed this same view of history, and in his thirty pages of introduction to Schaff's book wrote of history as movement, the ultimate tendency of which is forward, not backward. Sometimes false tendencies work themselves out through long experiments, perhaps of disastrous consequence. Nevertheless, the movement is onward; God's purposes in the Incarnation will not be denied even when the inclinations of humanity may seek to thwart those purposes.[44] This theology of history is possessed by an ecumenical and catholic spirit of wholeness that does not crusade against sects but reaches out in healing because the end result must come "in the way of historical development, self-mediated under God, and in a certain sense self-produced." The sectarian and Protestant minds "should be brought to see more and more the actual wants of the time, and thus be engaged to sigh and reach after the deliverance, which in that case might be supposed to be at hand."[45]

HISTORY: EPOCHS AND ERAS

A few years later, Nevin reviewed the year 1848 and its revolutionary activities. These events were ushering in a "new epoch" of history. Although the revolutionaries and their ideas may have been filled with false tendencies, they figured in the transition to a new historical era. The proper attitude in such times is neither that of radical revolution nor of conservative reaction. The incarnational movement of history requires a respectful loyalty to what has been achieved while remaining faithfully open to what is to come. The substance of life is stable and grounded, but never fixed.[46] In this essay Nevin introduced a use of the word "epoch" that remained a feature of his theology of history. The movement of history in the light of the Incarnation provided evidence of stages that revealed the character of its progressive development. An epoch is a time denoting marked change. We look back through the crises that faced us and observe what God has required of us and the manner in which our delusion and willfulness had to be overcome in order that the Kingdom could be advanced. History is always synthetic. Eucharistic participation in the Body of Christ endows the perception required to respond inwardly in a proper fashion to the outward events of the historical process in their providential potential. Epochs are the dramatic reminders of a reordering progress in development. Between epochs, said Nevin, are eras that lie there in such a way that there are no decided breaks, rather connections, between epochs. Every epoch carries an old era into a new one. The American Revolution was an epoch, a world epoch representing the grand reordering of history into an era in which universal history is envisioned and realized.[47] The crisis of 1848 was part of the American Epoch, the occasion in which European unrest and rebellion worked on behalf of liberty through the medium of American influence and in response to the theater of a new order that beckons in America. America was a new center for the sacred reconstitution of a New World—here Europe and Asia must join hands.[48]

THE INTERNAL AND EXTERNAL COURSE OF HISTORY

It is clear that Nevin's thought was effectively shaped in the direction of a theology of history. He rejected the seemingly pantheistic character of Hegel's philosophy because it seemed not to give due recognition to the need for human inward response to its own denial of the manifestation of God in history. History is no simple onslaught of divine possession and manipulation. After all, God in Christ was crucified, and although he rose from the dead, the rule of life in this world follows a pattern of death and resurrection. Nevin was probably influenced by Neander in his modification of the rationalism of the Hegelian dialectic. Hegelianism was rationalism to Nevin, and all rationalism is misplaced intelligence.[49] Neander had sought the way around Hegel's pantheism, and its undermining of the inward personal responsibility that was essential to the historical process, by grounding the notion of development in the experience that lies behind the formulation of dogma.[50]

The sense of history essential to Christianity imposed a certain historical responsibility upon human beings in their freedom. We were free to respond to the events that signal the reordering of existence. Freedom was expressed in imagination and faith. To be a historian, said Nevin, one must have poetic imagination, which is "the law of the universal idea of the world." In other words, imagination is the power to anticipate the sense of facts, the power to resuscitate that which would seem to be past, but is actually the awareness of duration brought about by human freedom. The human being is at once the center of that which is actual and ideal, universal and particular. The completeness of the human personality involves "comprehension in a life more general" than the individual separately considered.[51] This juxtaposition of ideal and actual, general and particular, is what distinguishes human existence from other forms of life. The human is able to imagine the wholeness in which we exist and have our being; this imagination works through reason and will to conceptualize and to take responsible actions that participate in the direction of human destiny in the world. Imagination is linked to freedom because "[i]t is the single will moving with self-conscious free activity in the orbit of the general will."[52] Freedom involves intelligence and the power of choice, according to Nevin, but this intelligence is more than rationality. It has to do with the sense of emergence "out of the night of nature" into a consciousness of the dual, but not contradictory, character of human existence. As such, intelligence would seem to be much more akin to Nevin's notion of imagination than to any analytical or calculating facility. The latter functions in service to intelligence as imagination.

Yet there is more to this intelligence than imagination. Faith, says Nevin, is necessary to the awareness and study of history. Faith is the ability to know that history is more than we make of it. Faith is the quality of recognized transcendence, the eye of insight that wills it to create history out of nature. In traditional language, faith knows that God is in history, that our consciousness of actual and ideal, general and particular, is the measure of our freedom to live in response to God. It is a recognition that we are created in the image of God. Imagination is image, the evidence of image in our perception, and is linked with faith in the human intelligence. Intelligence and the power of choice create history and are necessary to the understanding and study of history.

For Nevin Christ is the paradigm of divine imagination, the key to history.[53] Of course, here again Nevin may have worked with the imperialistic and triumphalist perspectives of the Christianity of his day. He may have associated his understanding of Christ too closely with the institutional fate of Christ's body in a sinful and competitive world.[54] Still, for Nevin, history is an objective enterprise as an object of study, even though our *knowledge* of history depends not merely on objective sources and resources but also on learning; but most of all on faith and imagination, which "reduce the crude material into a picture or counterpart of the true historical movement, as something that possesses in it a life truly organic."[55] The historian must be possessed of a standpoint, a center from which to view history. The center must be more than a private one; it must be a view of the whole being. History cannot be perceived simply by means of the laws of nature, which are the artifacts of observation of the natural mind. Only a center that is not reducible to merely natural laws can serve as the context in which faith and imagination interpret the course of events in "the economy of the whole."[56] Christ is that center, the Incarnation of wholeness that unlocks the mysteries and apparent contradictions of history. As some twentieth-century religious thinkers, such as Teilhard de Chardin and Paul Tillich, have shown, the understanding of Christ as center does not require a commitment to Christianity as superior religion. It may require the Church to manifest in sacramental fashion the reality of the compassionate Christ whose suffering and death are followed by a resurrection that reminds us that the divine movement of history will not be ultimately thwarted. "The Universal Christ," wrote Teilhard, "is a synthesis of Christ and the universe. He is not a new godhead—but an inevitable deployment of the mystery in which Christianity is summed up, the mystery of the Incarnation."[57] Somehow, I find this not out of harmony with the spirit of John Nevin's theology of history.

six

"A THEATRE FOR THE WORLD": NATIONALISM AND THE AMERICAN REPUBLIC

In the critical year 1848, John Nevin reflected on the events that were occurring here and abroad:

> When we read in the present state of the world, the approach of a new historical period, whose character and course are to be determined prevailingly by the new order of life which reigns in America, we are not so foolish as to conceive of this under the form of a simple triumph of our national spirit, as it now stands, over the political institutions of the old world. . . . The revolutionary spirit of the age [has its significance] in the yet undeveloped life toward which transitionally it points and leads. This lies in the direction which the course of history has already begun to take in America . . . by means of the theatre here opened.[1]

Nevin rejected the spirit of nationalism that emerged on this side of the Atlantic during the early decades of the nineteenth century. It was but a "sophomorical style of self-gratification" and tended to think of America "as a settled and given fact" rather than as a theater for a new order of world history.[2] "The day for 'Nativism,' in all its forms, is fast drawing to an end," wrote Nevin in his extraordinary analysis entitled "The Year 1848."[3] The spirit of catholicity and the understanding of history that Nevin brought to the analysis of public circumstances required a metaphor quite unlike the "city upon a hill" so prominent in the rhetorical consciousness of Puritan America.

For John Nevin, America was a "theatre for the world," not a "city upon a hill." It was not a fixed and settled empire but a stage provided for the enactment of a new world epoch. America was a theater of becoming, not a place chosen, like a "little Israel" already established for the world to see and

envy. There was a nationalistic spirit at work in America, a spirit that threatened its very world-historical significance. Nationalism is a kind of exclusiveness, which "dreams itself in possession already of the 'celestial empire,' and
can only commiserate or despise the barbarian world that lies beyond."[4]

As a theater for the world, America must not wall out the life of the
world in its many forms but must be constantly inclusive, making room for
and taking onto its stage the living economy of the world. The great cultural
achievements of Europe are not accomplishments of the past alone, now su-
perseded or replaced by "American" success. Europe has not yet completed
her part in the great drama taking place. Nor is Europe to be set aside as a
grand failure and America to be the fixed city, the celestial empire. America
is a theater for the drama of wholeness to take on a new form.[5] Here we see
Nevin's concept of catholicity at work. The Kingdom announced and made
present in the Incarnation—the Kingdom has come; but it is a dynamic reality
bringing "a character of universal *wholeness* and completeness . . . a process
of growth; and the circumstances of [America] make it impossible to bind this
process to any outward lines or limits."[6]

THE STAGE IS SET

In this theater there is place for the organization of a new order of life, not to
be claimed or possessed but to reach beyond its limits, always expressing a
wholeness greater than limited achievement or understanding. "We cannot
speak of our American nationality as a settled and given fact, in the same way
that we may speak of the nationality of England or France."[7] There is, of
course, a sense of American destiny at work in Nevin's thought. However, the
emergence of the American Republic is unique evidence of the providential
ordering of history, not in some deterministic manner but as a theater, an
opportunity for something new to be made manifest. The success of this new
world epoch will depend on the internal response of the people to the outward working of history. American nationalism cannot be nation-ism; it must
represent something new. It must be open, not closed or fixed. Therein is its
unique "nationalistic" destiny.

American citizens in the first half of the nineteenth century were caught
up in the swelling tides of mission and manifest destiny. The spirit of the new
nation was empowered by a sense of pride and independence, an adolescent
perception of boundless power and energy. Newspaper editorials waxed prophetic as they predicted ever-increasing incidents of revolutions in Europe in
the throes of Old World decay. A form of expansionism took shape in

America, born of anxiety for those people still in chains in other lands and concerned that other peoples might not be able to accept their own democratic destiny without our help. Winthrop Hudson called this expansionism a form of "continentalism" bred by the vision of a vast continent waiting to be settled and developed through the millennial expectations of Evangelical religion.[8] America was a new nation in a revolutionary world. Europeans were watching from across the waters; they had seen the light in the sky and from the depth of their own darkness had begun to throw off their chains. In 1848 the continental expansionism of many Americans was frustrated by the stubbornness of Mexicans and the Whig opposition to this form of nationalism.

BEYOND PARTY SPIRIT

Nevin was neither Whig nor Democrat in this matter. His rejection of party spirit as inimical to social and political order prevented this. He may have reflected the Federalist posture of the turn of the century, but there were Democratic aspects of his agenda, as well as an abhorrence of the individualism so evident in sectarian religion and the Jeffersonian legacy. But, as James Bratt has put it:

> How could the Whigs have it both ways: growth, individual willfulness, sectarian multiplication on the one hand, and organic harmony, stable order on the other? As for the Democrats, how long could white and ethnic liberties live beside black slavery; and how could a simple, face-to-face society of local rights survive the national expansion and economic development that this party also hailed?[9]

A republic must not depend on party spirit to maintain itself, according to Nevin. Party spirit is sectarianism and leads to little more than exclusive posturing designed to vindicate the correctness of private judgment. Human beings are not what they were even a century prior to the 1840s. The social principle, said Nevin, is what makes us human; it points to a wholeness in which individuals exist. This wholeness constantly works to bring together "the dissevered elements of humanity."

> Party spirit is an abuse, a misdirection of the social principle. It employs it but only for its own selfish purposes and ends. Its professions, of course, are always good, or they try to appear so. Not seldom the objects sought to be promoted are in themselves commendable, but both the spirit and the means employed in their pursuit are totally foreign to their nature. The partisan cares most for himself. . . . Most malicious, satanic and vile is this Spirit of

Party, under whatever place it shows itself, whether in high places of the Church, State, or elsewhere. . . . The mischief and evils flowing from Party spirit, when it once gets possession of the social principle, and perverts it in the interest of pure individual selfishness, extend over the entire surface of human life, everywhere blighting what is good and true as a malignant mildew.[10]

From the perspective of the realism of American politics, we may wish to believe that Nevin's critique of political parties is little more than an idealistic tirade. We have learned to accept the necessity of a party system, partly because we regard it as the most pragmatic way of facilitating a government that avoids extremes and prevents the tyranny of the majority. Yet when we reflect on the intransigence of party politics in our own day, we may wish to reassess Nevin's ideas on the subject. It is not difficult to note that the party spirit subordinates the public interest. Parties respond to the legislative appeals of presidential leadership with rhetoric derived from little concern other than the well-being and authority of the parties themselves. Subsequently they accuse each other of partisan politics. Although some of this posturing helps to avoid the pitfalls of hasty solution, it also prevents the advancement of what Nevin called the social principle. The latter principle is a foretaste, an earnest, of the wholeness represented in the Incarnation. In a sense, it is a visitation of that wholeness. The American Republic must depend for its future on the transcendence of party spirit, which is the individualism rampant in our national soul. A republic must remain in communion with the great and good of all ages, said Nevin. It must be sustained by the presence of catholicity, as it works among the noblest of human aspirations or achievements. Whether they are aware of the mind of Plato or the spirit of those motivated by the gospel, the American people must be nurtured by a catholicity that is essential to the fashioning of the Republic. Nevin suggested the example of George Washington as true republican patriot who accomplished more for us as one who rose above party spirit than he accomplished in war.[11]

WORLD-HISTORICAL DRAMA

John Nevin was not a revolutionary. He did not champion human causes, because that kind of action implied that humanity in its natural condition could claim the fullness of truth about the course of history. For Nevin, history was the result of human response to world-historical circumstances that often were outward manifestations of providential ordering. Therefore, revolutions like those of the 1840s might be evidence of the need for effective and discerning response to the great social change that had been made possible by America as "theatre for the world." But, for him, the revolutionary spirit rampant in Europe was entitled "to no sort of confidence or respect. In its own constitution, it is from beneath rather than from above; and the work accordingly, which it is pretending to accomplish, may not be expected to stand. Its significance is not so much in itself, as in the yet undeveloped life towards which transitionally it points and leads."[12] In other words, the world was not without sense or reason *before* the revolutions of 1848. Monarchy is not identical with tyranny, nor is American republican nationalism to be equated with freedom. The Providence of God is not driving kings from thrones and lifting up America as the "city upon a hill"—the most perfect exemplification of liberty. This kind of speculation is narrow sectarianism, elevated in party spirit to the kind of nationalism that has held the world captive. It equates its own natural inclinations and insights with the wisdom of God, which in its revealed catholicity calls us to ever more inclusive and universal moments than the present can envision.

Nevin does not spell out the relationship of Christian faith to the dynamics of republican political and social order. However, there is enough available of the structure of his thought for us to make confident inference. He has provided us with the substance of his catholic theology and his theology of history. Theology, for Nevin, is not ideology.[13] Therefore, it offers no blueprint for social and political change. Instead, his theology offers both the insight and the faith and imagination necessary for appropriate and continuing response to the movement of history. At the heart of this response is the mystical presence of Christ communicated in the Eucharist. The Eucharist allows us to live open to change, without dependence on "mere insular traditions," yet recognizing the incorporation of "the sense of the universal past."[14] The Church of the future will not be the Church of the present because Christ's presence includes full humanity as well as divinity. Therefore, something is constantly being brought to pass in the course of history itself. "History, like nature, is one vast prophecy of the incarnation, from beginning to end."[15] No human entity, regarded in its merely naturalistic and rationalistic sense, is a perfect reality but is subject to the dynamics of wholeness which the Incarnation represents and "prophesies" (to use Nevin's word). Therefore, the Church changes, too, in keeping with the epochs of history.

THE CONSTITUTION AND "THE CONSTITUTION"

In the theater of the world represented by the American Republic, the Church is important also as the vital force that nurtures and guarantees the

constitution of virtue essential to republican life. Robert Bellah has called attention to Montesquieu's notion that the principle of social life basic to a republic
is virtue.[16] Presumably every society is *constituted* by a set of ideas, values,
beliefs, and practices that reflect its perception of reality. We may refer to this
"set" as the constitution of virtue that makes a republic possible. During the
late eighteenth and early nineteenth centuries, the constitution of European
and Euro-American life was in the process of alteration. A republican constitution was in the making. In the American theater, the process was revolutionary in nature. The shaping of society in colonial America was revolutionary in character, altering the constitution of human nature and the social order
in the direction of liberty and equality. The revelation was well under way to
success before the War of Independence was fought.

This line of reasoning reminds us that the formal Constitution, the document of American mythic provenance, was possible in a theater of the world
where a constitution of republican virtue and experience already existed.[17] It
would seem wise for us to remember this when, in our own latter days, we
seek to impose republican governance and its attendant constitutions upon
peoples of the world for whom no such constitution is viable. Presumably a
constitution of republican virtue is likely to emerge where people exist in a
landscape that is spacious, where breaking boundaries is easy, and where the
economic well-being of people is assured by hard work and stubbornness. Asia
and Europe are places where geographical, social, and cultural boundaries are
transgressed only at great cost.

Relying on this notion of what I have called the constitution of republican virtue and experience, Robert Bellah has argued that such a constitution
as this requires constant nurturing.[18] Otherwise, the nation becomes a republican simulacrum, held together by a facade of legal technique. The Constitution becomes a mechanistic device, almost fetishistic in its function. Or perhaps, what is even more ominous in modern times, the nation is maintained
by the authoritarian structures of technocorporate systems while Constitutional and legal maneuvering permit us to retain the illusion of democratic
republicanism.

As I have shown in an earlier chapter, Bellah has suggested that the sustaining element in the early Republic was the biblical tradition as it was played
out in the work of Evangelical Protestantism. It was this biblical tradition, said
Bellah, that helped us to avoid the kind of utilitarian individualism associated
with John Locke and Thomas Hobbes. "Rooted ultimately in the sophistic,
skeptical, and hedonistic strands of ancient Greek philosophy," the modern
form "believed in a neutral state in which individuals would be allowed to
pursue the maximization of their self-interest and the product would be public
and private prosperity."[19] Utilitarian individualism concentrated on "the ratio-

nalization of means, or technical reason"; it had no interest in a community of shared values or goals. Self-restraint and morality were utilitarian means to self-interest. Bellah recognized that the "biblical tradition" and utilitarian individualism operated side by side as "interpretations of reality in America"; and that a harmonization of the two occurred because the former was corrupted by the latter.[20] Here he is in agreement with John Nevin, who maintained that the form of religiousness most common to the new nation was a false or pseudo-Protestantism. The powerful forces of revivalistic Evangelicalism had recognized the utilitarian value of their own assumptions and practices for the rising individual.

False Protestantism was Christian faith in service to "Bible and private judgment"—the twin principles of sectarianism.[21] These principles fashioned what Sidney Mead has called a "prevailing Protestant ideology [which] represented a syncretistic mingling of the . . . religion of the denominations, which was commonly articulated in terms of scholastic Protestant orthodoxy and almost universally practiced in terms of the experimental religion of pietistic revivalism [and] the religion of the democratic society and nation."[22]

Charles Finney and Lyman Beecher played variations on this same theme but assumed that some version of pietistic revivalism was essential to the life of the young Republic, supplying it with the harmony and moral tonality of its composition. Bellah has suggested that an uncorrupted element of the Evangelical religion and its "prevailing Protestant ideology" continued to nurture the nation, to maintain the constitution of virtue essential to the continuation of the Republic. The outward Constitution was viable because the inner constitution was maintained by uncorrupted Evangelical religion. What shall the Republic do, asks Bellah, now that the Evangelical tradition is no longer able to guarantee the constitution of virtue? Modernity has taken it toll, and radical pluralism and secularism have rendered Evangelicalism dysfunctional as a "prevailing . . . ideology."

John Nevin would have said that the Evangelical tradition was ineffective because it was another form of utilitarian individualism. The principle of Bible and private judgment were both the product and continuing progenitors of religious self-interest. Revivalism as a primary mode of religious advocacy was the maximization of self-interest. This was what Nicolas Berdyaev, in the twentieth century, was to call transcendental egoism:

> [T]he idea of the exclusive concern for the salvation of one's own soul . . . is a satanic idea, a satanic caricature of Christianity. In truth only he saves his soul who is ready to lose it for the sake of his fellow men, in the name of Christ's love. We must not think about our own salvation; this is a wrong state of mind, and is heavenly utilitarianism.[23]

According to Nevin, this "heavenly utilitarianism" and its "transcendental egoism" tended toward a self-righteous concern for salvation as "something comparatively outward to the proper life," a mechanism for saving us from hell and leading us to maximize our spiritual self-interest by assuring ourselves of flight from the wrath to come and by helping as many others, separately considered, to the same end. But, said Nevin, the wholeness of the Kingdom of God breaks all preconceived boundaries of selfhood and is extended to cover the field of being at all points, with no constituent interest or relationship taken "as extrinsical ever to its rightful domain." [24] The twin principles of Bible and private judgment were the axioms of "heavenly utilitarianism" and the sect spirit. They could hardly be expected to nurture the constitution of republican virtue, yet they represented the prevailing American religiousness.

As Sacvan Bercovitch writes,

> Consider the alternative claims upon the promise [of a "shining city on a hill"] by the self-reliant individual and the self-proclaimed nation of individualism. In that conflict lies a central cultural contradiction: the threat of society inherent in the very ideals of self-interest through which society justifies itself. . . . [T]he rhetoric implies that America's future, and by extension the fate of humanity, hinges on the efforts of the individual representative American. [25]

The American Republic was a new political creation, a theater for the world; it required a radical catholic spirit. Instead it was being nurtured by a spirit of heavenly utilitarianism that reified the "city upon a hill" as another form of nationalism.

NO ABSTRACT AMERICANISM

From Nevin's perspective in the essay "The Year 1848," America had to avoid a kind of New World nationalism, which was merely a triumphalist version of the nationalist impulse rampant in Europe, with the possible distinction derived from a vision of America as a chosen, covenanted nation. New World nationalism was an extension of the same principle at work in utilitarian individualism, a nationalism that is the collectivization of individual expectations—no greater wholeness than the abstract allness of national and sectarian illusion. In this view the nation was simply the contractual and voluntary association of individuals who will work out their destiny by the maximization of self-interest. Individual claims and expectations become the utilitarian measure of all goodness; the common good, the national good, is the magnification of the individual's pursuit of happiness. However, naked nationalism is as much an abstraction as naked individualism.

As Nevin was to make clear in his essay "Catholicism," the idea of catholicity as a universal "allness" was a distortion and abstraction of the essential character of universality. "Allness" represents a collectivity that is very limited and finite. Allness is, in fact, secondary to the individual existences from which it is abstracted; it is a process that begins with single things and by comparison and abstraction is raised to what is supposedly general.[26] Allness is a very modern, perhaps American, concept—which does not mean, of course, that it may not have its counterparts in the new nationalistic and revolutionary thinking of Europe. Allness becomes a substitute for wholeness and distorts religious and political thought and action. It encourages sectarianism, which is a religious equivalent to nationalism.

The whole person is more than the aggregation of empirically constituent parts; the whole of nature is more than the summation of objects that may be observed and measured at any given time; and the whole of humanity is more than all individuals of any one or all generations. Presumably, a people or a "nation" is more than the collectivity of individuals within a territorial space. This is what Nevin had identified in 1849 as "abstract Americanism."[27] The latter perceives itself as a closed empirical entity, a "city upon a hill," the eyes of all the world upon it. It is an abstraction like utilitarian individualism, failing to understand the creative context in which it exists. It disregards the fact that the American Republic is not a fixed entity, but as an

> incorporation of the true substance of history from all sides . . . it is not enough that the outward material of the nation be gathered from all lands; it must take up into its inward constitution also, what is of worth in the mind and heart of all lands; so as to be, not merely a mixture of the several reigning nationalities, but an inward reproduction of their true sense under a new organic and universal form.[28]

Abstract Americanism does not recognize the openness of reality, the wholeness in which it participates. Instead, it wishes to emphasize its separateness, its abstraction from the general substance of history that gives it root. The twin principles of Bible and private judgment have their likeness in the history-less nationalism and rationalism of the political order. In contrast, the American Republic as theater for the world does not support the supposition that other nations have completed their parts in the drama, or even that their continuing significance requires a confession of

> their whole past to have been a lie [requiring them] to take a fresh start politically, in the footsteps of the American republic. . . . Europe is not to

be set aside as a grand failure. The true wealth of her past life will be carried forward to the new state, in which her institutions are to be finally perfected in their own form, by means of this crisis [of the year 1848].[29]

The American Republic is something really new, according to Nevin. Abstract Americanism and history-less sectarianism were aberrations, distortions of what was actually happening in the world. As long as they continued, they would impede the potential course of history and work against the dialectical power of Providence. The true source of nurture for the constitution of virtue that was essential to republican continuity was not maximized self-interest, either nationally or spiritually, but the celebration of the mystical presence. "The mystery of the incarnation involves in itself potentially a new order of existence for the world, which is as universal in its own nature as the idea of humanity, and by which only it is possible for this to be advanced finally to its full and perfect realization."[30] This mystery is the perception of wholeness rather than allness; it is a form of knowing that enables us to perceive reality from the perspective of its wholeness rather than of abstract utilitarian individualism. Humanity is never complete in itself, either separately considered or collectively mustered. Humanity points to Christ; it exhibits in its very constitution the form of wholeness made present in Christ.

UTILITARIAN CHRISTIANITY

The sectarian mind, in its religious and political contours, ignores the wholeness that is mystically present by way of the Incarnation. It is left to its own meager vision and resource. It is a utilitarian mind, claiming that maximal private judgment rewards the individual with the assurance of truth and goodness. "Our national credo," writes Henry May, "has often been described as a combination of simple moral maxims and easy utilitarianism."[31] To the extent that May's observation is correct, it is an indication of the fact that Nevin's insight into our republican dilemma went unheeded. Maximized self-interest has won out, and nothing exists to sustain the virtue essential to guarantee the constitution that makes the Constitution meaningful—in which case the latter exists as an external document attempting to manage the lives of abstract individuals in an abstract American nation.

In his study *Individualism and Public Life,* Ralph Ketcham reminds us that "Americans have tended to see their freedom and fulfillment as proportionate to their lack of public burden and intrusion."[32] Although it is not easy for American intellectuals and scholars to admit it, the popular mind of America is still effectively shaped by the revivalistic Evangelical tradition of Christianity, a tradition that also reflects the utilitarian individualism of the culture. The churches have become collectivities of individual spiritual self-interest. And inasmuch as the church is thereby reduced to utilitarian significance, individuals project their individualistic perceptions onto a screen of nationalistic collectivity as well. In this sense neither Church nor state represents more than collective self-interest, individually considered. Both are mechanical and abstract realities. As Nevin had pointed out in his diatribe against Finney's "New Measures":

> The higher force does not strictly and properly take possession of the lower, but is presumed to have been reduced to the possession and service of this last, to be used by it for its own convenience. Religion does not get the sinner, but it is the sinner who gets "religion." Justification is taken to be in fact by *feeling,* not by faith; and in this way falls back . . . into the sphere of self-righteousness.[33]

In other words, when the person is reduced to the proportions of his own expectations, he is abstracted from the context that makes him a person. The resulting abstract individual then seeks to take possession of whatever will serve its ends. The wholeness that the Incarnation embodies is then reduced to a "feeling," a conversion experience that one can "get." This, in Nevin's understanding, meant a justification by feeling, rather than by faith as response to the "higher force." A revival, said Finney, is a "purely philosophical result of the right use of constituted means."[34] It is "getting" religion. Nevin's was a revolutionary discovery in American religious thought; he had discovered that American fascination with individual salvation was a distortion of the Christian gospel. The catholic character of that "good news" about the impact of the Incarnation on the world had direct implication for social and cultural understanding. It is, therefore, inadequate to reduce Nevin's theology to a mere American counterpart to the "traditionalist, 'churchly,' sacramental" romanticism that swept across Europe "in the second generation of the nineteenth century."[35] Nevin's discovery was traumatic for him; it led to his "five years of dizziness,"[36] the period of his life in which the claims of the Roman Church made considerable sense.

Nevin's understanding of the catholic character of the gospel had much in common with the organic views of Horace Bushnell, expressed in *Christian Nurture*. In an extended review of the latter work that appeared in several issues of the *Weekly Messenger* during June and July of 1847, Nevin expressed great appreciation for Bushnell's assertion of the "organic, historical nature of religion" as over against the abstract individualism of the American Christianity of the day. However, in Nevin's thinking, Bushnell was unable to come to terms with the doctrine of the Church as the context in which faith is nurtured and expressed. Bushnell's church is based upon the constitution of nature, in Nevin's view, "rather than upon the constitution of grace" as a new creation present in the historical realm. Bushnell's argument is finally rationalistic, said Nevin, and therefore defective,[37] because Bushnell was unable to rise above the privatism he seemed to deplore in his organic understanding of life. His educational religion lays no supernatural foundation for the transformation of culture beyond the common life of individuals intent upon being educated and nurtured.[38]

For John Nevin, both the state and the Church are greater than the sum of their parts. To the extent that the Church is free to be in this world as the Body of Christ, celebrating the mystical presence of the Incarnation, it provides the insight into and resource for taking up "the living economy of the world more and more into" the reign of Christ.[39] America has a role to play in this Heilsgeschichte. The state is not a "factitious or accidental institution . . . continued for the use of man's life from abroad and brought near to it only in an outward manner."[40] The state belongs inherently to life. It is an organic expression of the moral nature, part of the activity of reason and will that is fundamental to existence. Although they belong to the organic constitution of nature, states derive their power and existence from the inherent necessity of their moral nature and their potential for expressing the wholeness that is present in human existence itself. Of course, states may try to usurp wholeness on behalf of their vision of allness as an extension of their individual needs. In so doing they attempt to convert their role as agencies in the moral order into extensions of pride and self-interest individually but collectively extended. This is nationalism, utilitarian individualism abstractly projected into organic pretension. It is the kind of "abstract Americanism" to which the new Republic must not fall victim.

THE NATION'S SECOND BIRTH

According to Nevin, the Civil War was "the nation's second birth." So he spoke of it at its close in 1865. Perhaps the rhetoric of Abraham Lincoln lingered in his memory, as it did in the minds of other Americans. His friendship with James Buchanan was not an exercise in party spirit that eliminated his appreciation for Lincoln, whom Nevin recognized as a servant of Providence who had "a sense of uncertain dependence upon the course of events."[41] Nevin's lecture echoes with the watchwords of Lincoln's speeches and his understanding of the providential balance of the circumstances of war and the tendency to justify the partisan feelings in both sides of the conflict. "If it be the province of tragedy to teach by subduing and mellowing the minds of men," said Nevin, "the martyrdom of Mr. Lincoln, taken in all its circumstances, may easily be seen to have been in this view a salutary discipline of the entire country."[42] That martyrdom challenges the nation to understand the struggle as Lincoln had. The chief magistrate had known that something profoundly providential was at work. Now the matter had been resolved historically. Old party issues are done away with, continued Nevin: "Let the dead bury the dead, the past sleep with the past. We plant ourselves here on the broad foundation of the world-historical present."[43]

There are nations, said Nevin, that are representative, like those representative persons who from time to time appear, incarnating the genius and spirit of human aspiration. Representative nations take into their existence the central stream of history. In passing through the recent political struggle, this nation had been playing a distinctive role in the drama of universal history. As a theater for the world, the American nation gave voice not merely to its own internal strife but also to forces at work in determining "the course and destiny of the world's life in a universal or whole view."[44] The Civil War was part of the movement of world history (Weltgeschichte).

What Nevin called "the grand leading epochs" of our earlier American life were part of the *first* birth of the nation. The social, political, and technological circumstances of Europe in the fifteenth and sixteenth centuries, the exploration of the New World, the European settlement of the North American continent, the Declaration of Independence, and the War of Independence were all epochs in the first birth of the nation. The Fourth of July of 1865 was unlike previous celebrations, invested as it was with the full power of its symbolic, world-historical significance. "It is not too much to say, what we should all thankfully feel, that the second birth of the nation here is far more glorious than the first."[45]

That was because, in Nevin's view, the nation had experienced resurrection. It had risen from the dead, from a conflict that made no sense, that had been entered into blindly, and that had continued for four years to represent the most diabolical of human characteristics and motives. The course and end of the war had been "so largely not only beyond, but even against, the sense and purpose of the powers that [had] been employed to bring it to pass."[46] The circumstances of the conflict demonstrated no great wisdom on the part of anyone; they were, in fact, so filled with "human corruption and error, to say nothing of Satanic wickedness," that the outcome was a miracle, a resurrection—the second birth of the nation. The sympathies of other nations, informed by the political philosophy of ages, had been against the plans and strategies of President Lincoln and the cause of the Union. The people of the world had looked on unbelievingly as great numbers of American citizens sought to avoid armed service at any cost. The *Times* of London affirmed the waning of the star of early American greatness. They should all have been proven correct in their gloomy predictions, said Nevin; the weight of past experience and historical analogy were indeed on their side. That matters turned out otherwise was a truly remarkable and providential legacy.

> The agony of the nation's second birth is over. The judgment of history, which is here plainly also the voice of God, has been spoken. We have gained what we believe to be a higher platform and plane for our political life. In this respect old things have passed away; let us work together now with united heart and hand, that all things may become new.[47]

The nation was becoming the theater for the working out of a "properly universal spirit." What was now at stake was a gathering up of the *inward constitution,* "what is of worth in the mind and heart of all lands," so that the outcome is "an inward reproduction of their true sense under a new organic and universal form."[48] Like the year 1848, the end of the Republic's minority, the nation's second birth was not a representation of old nationalisms but a world-historical event.

Nevin's rejection of the salvational self-interest present in revivalistic Evangelicalism is of a piece with his denial of abstract Americanism. The Bible-and-private-judgment sectarianism of the former is the same principle at work in a sectarian and utilitarian nationalism that thinks of the Republic as a voluntary association of individuals maximizing their own self-interest and set apart from the rest of the world in collective pride. As a theater for the world, the nation has been given a further or a second chance. Perhaps the war had occurred because the Republic had failed to take into its inward constitution what Providence had been offering in the crisis of 1848. Perhaps it had been engaged too much in the furtherance of its sectarian interests. If so, Providence had provided a new occasion, fashioning the opportunity for a representative nation to "take up into [itself] and show forth . . . beyond others, the central stream of history, regarded as being for the world at large. . . ."[49]

seven

BEYOND SECTARIAN MISSIONS

In an essay entitled "Catholicism," John Nevin wrote:

At this very time it is of more account, that the power of Christianity should be wrought intensively into the whole civilization of this country (the weight of which prospectively no one can fully estimate); that it should have in it not merely an outward and nominal sovereignty, but be brought also fully to actuate and inform its interior collective life . . . for the bringing in of the millenium [sic], than the conversion of all India or China. The life of the Church is the salvation of the world.[1]

More recently, Martin E. Marty has observed:

To many people the most dazzling and the most puzzling achievement was the ability of evangelicals to keep their eye on the West and the world at the same moment. Starting from a small base in the population, preoccupied with surviving and developing forms and theology, they were concerned not to see the empire divided spiritually between home and foreign mission.[2]

The minds of many Americans in the early nineteenth century were charged with images of millions of hopeless mortals "rushing through pagan darkness . . . down to hopeless death."[3] The empire of benevolent societies, directed by Christian laypersons intent upon rescuing the perishing, opened their hearts and purses to a world that summoned forth contrition for past exploitation and compassion for hungry and unregenerate souls. Most Americans derived their understanding of other peoples and their cultures through the mediation of missionary rhetoric that dominated the American pulpit and the articles in countless denominational newspapers. Colporteurs distributed pamphlets and books that shaped the thinking of public life. Even the regular newspapers were frequent disseminators of the prevailing religious perceptions of Americans. It is probably safe to say that missionary rhetoric was the most pervasive source of cross-cultural understanding, even of international relations.[4] International understanding and policy continued to be shaped by missionary rhetoric until well into the twentieth century.

America, after all, was the "land promised to the saints", and here was to be the focus of the consummation of history. Centuries of speculation about the land across the waters to the west had energized European thinking and invested this continent with the religious status of a New World. The suffering, oppression, and immorality of the Old World would be overcome. A new historical age would dawn in America. Jonathan Edwards wrote:

> 'Tis not unlikely that this work of God's Spirit [the Great Awakening], that is so extraordinary and wonderful, is the dawning, or at least a prelude, of that glorious work of God, so often foretold in Scripture, which in the progress and issue of it, shall renew the world of mankind. If we consider how long since the things foretold, as what should precede this great event, have been accomplished; and how long this event has been expected by the Church of God, and thought to be nigh by the most eminent men of God in the Church; and withal consider what the state of things now is, and has for a considerable time been, in the Church of God and world of mankind, we can't reasonably think otherwise, than that the beginning of this great work of God must be near, and there are many things that make it probable that this work will begin in America.[5]

MISSIONS AND ESCHATOLOGY

What were Americans to make of this eschatological view of their role in world history? Some of them were to interpret it as an imminent apocalyptic expectation and attach to it the "sentiment that since Christ was so soon to return and reign with His saints, only a few years remained for preaching the gospel to the whole world and for gathering souls into the fold."[6] Edwards's eschatology refused to confine itself to an exclusively political goal. He had directed his thinking against any pride in America and fixed his vision on a transcendent reality that critiques all earthly kingdoms. However, the imminent adventists were not so sober and theologically skilled as Edwards. They invested their hopes, as R. Pierce Beaver informs us, in a sentimental turn of mind in which they could have pity for perishing heathen and work feverishly at the "plucking of brands from the burning."[7] Eschatology was the motive for mission. Whether one held the sober, transcendent views of Edwards or the sentimental perspectives of the imminentists, the effect was almost the same. Somehow, it was difficult for most Americans to maintain Edwards's sophistication; and the utilitarian individualism nourished by Hobbes and the Enlightenment made common cause with the tendency to reduce theological themes to manageable rational and political ends.

By the nineteenth century it became difficult to sort out the subtle differences between Edwards's ideas and the notions of imminentists and the political eschatology of Lyman Beecher and the heralds of revivalism. Revivals are things we make happen, said Charles Grandison Finney. And so Americans became virtually obsessed with the vision of rescuing every perishing soul on the face of the planet. Thus, in the utilitarian mind of America, eschatology became politicized. It has motivated an agenda in which America is to *accomplish* the renovation of the world by doing what Finney would have approved—making conversions happen. What should serve as a critique of the social order becomes in effect the sanction for efforts to socialize *all* the people of the world by means of Christian salvation. The *wholeness* that was communicated in a more healthy eschatology was sacrificed to *allness.*

MISSIONS IN VOCATIONAL PERSPECTIVE

In 1843, the year of the first edition of *The Anxious Bench* and three years into the Mercersburg period, John Nevin addressed the problem of missions. In keeping with the spirit of the times, the German Reformed Church was involved in the great American cause of Evangelical benevolence on behalf of the missionary enterprise. The question of home missions was being raised because of the increased impact of immigration on the American denominations. This was an especial concern for the small denomination which Nevin served as a theologian. Many of the immigrants were German, a fact that presented renewed responsibility for German Americans. It is interesting to note that this issue promoted a certain form of ecumenicity that paralleled the common lay Christianity of the benevolent empire. For example, Lutheran and Reformed churches tried to fashion a cooperative response to German immigrants that centered in a kind of ethnic Christianity. Just as the German Reformed Church participated in a *Reformed* partnership with the Dutch Reformed Church and the Presbyterians, they were also at work with fellow Germans in the Lutheran connection.

Foreign mission work had begun in earnest in the early nineteenth century, sparked by the frontier spirit and the eschatological mood of America's laity. The American Board of Commissioners for Foreign Missions had been founded in 1810, growing out of the "haystack prayer meeting" at Williams College in 1806. In 1843, however, the concern was for "home missions." People are not the same; they do not all have the same vocation, said Nevin. The exercise of benevolent giving and action hangs in the delicate balance of a divine economy that expects different efforts at different times, all directed by particular vocational responsibilities. Just as individuals do not all have the same vocation, so also a Christian community is expected "to consider what the will of the Lord concerning it may be, as it regards the general work of the Gospel, and to lay out its strength accordingly."[8] The Christian community in America is currently charged with the special vocation of addressing its home missionary efforts to the welfare of immigrants. No other interest, said Nevin, is so momentous. It forms the present mandate for the Church in America.[9]

According to Nevin, a principle of vocational selection had been at work in the policy of *foreign* missions—a principle that was somewhat at odds with the assumptions behind much Evangelical thinking. The utilitarian salvation of revivalism was supposedly concerned with the enlargement of the Church, understood as an eschatological amassment of *all* the souls in the world. Presumably this assumption would lead to feverish and random wholesale activity, making "additions mechanically brought into connection with [the Church] from without rather than by the extension of its own organic life from within."[10] Yet foreign missionary stations had been selected, said Nevin, with a vocational sense that made certain particular lands and peoples a matter of extreme significance. Policy was shaped and care was taken, "with reference to the future as well as the present, and with an eye not simply to the value of a certain number of souls immediately to be reached . . . but to interests immensely more comprehensive, which are felt to lie beyond."[11]

FORMING THE MIND OF CHRIST IN THE AMERICAN THEATER

It is this principle of vocational selection that affects the need for home missionary efforts on behalf especially of the German immigrants. Although the numerical extent of immigrant additions to the New World population is itself a factor hardly to be dismissed, there is, continued Nevin a "moral point of view." A "mind" is being formed as the immigrants enter the American scene. How shall that mind be shaped? How shall it grow? Shall it belong to Christ or Antichrist? Nevin does not define Antichrist in this context, and one wonders whether it is to be equated with sectarianism or the dark side of the human condition. There is little doubt, however, said Nevin, that the mission-

ary shaping of this "mind" in the American setting is of much greater significance than "the conversion of all China or of all Africa to Christianity." That
is because, as we saw in the last chapter, America, according to Nevin, is a
theater for the world.

Five years prior to his theological discussion of American nationalism,
reflected in the essay "The Year 1848," Nevin was already anticipating the
ideas that took constructive form in relation to revivalism, the missionary task,
and the holistic presence of the Incarnation in history. Because the Kingdom
must come in the vast cultural traditions of an evolving humanity, the principle of vocational selection requires intensification of missionary efforts within
the American theater. "This is felt by the nations generally," he wrote in 1843.
"The eyes of Europe are turned towards our shores, with an expectation that
becomes more wakeful and anxious every year. The destinies of the world are
seen more and more to be suspended on the course of events here."[12] The
völkerwanderungen represented in the American theater is world-historical, a
way of redirecting history toward a greater catholicity. A new mind has to be
formed in America, as a result of this great shift of populations. What is involved is not a mere collectivity of individuals but a mind that is nurtured by
the mystical presence of Christ.

The German Reformed Church in America has a special vocational mandate with regard to this sacramental commission. Nations differ constitution-
ally in intellectual and moral character. As the constitution of the American
mind is being shaped, the German character is full of promise, said Nevin.
The German mind is naturally serious and profound; "[i]t seeks communion
with the inward rather than the outward."[13] That is an especially efficacious
quality as American religion seeks to overcome the utilitarian individualism
and salvationism of the American mind with its concern for external evidence
of quantitative success.

Nevin did not agree with the notion of total depravity promulgated by
certain interpreters of Calvin. As Luther Binkley has pointed out: "The orthodox Calvinistic view is that the decree of election preceded and governed
the creation and fall of man."[14] Or, as Brian Gerrish has interpreted Nevin:
"Though he reached back—behind 'puritanism'—to a more authentically
Calvinistic tradition, in the end he did not want the whole Calvin any more
than Princeton. And if Hodge ceded Calvin's eucharistic theology to Mercersburg, Nevin gladly let Princeton keep the Calvin of the 'horrible decree.'"[15] For, as Nevin was to make clear in *The Mystical Presence* (1846), and
later in "The Doctrine of the Reformed Church on the Lord's Supper"
(1850), God did not find the order of the natural world to be inimical to the
divine economy. The Incarnation effects a real union between the divine and

the human (and natural). In his discussion entitled "The Church Year," he stresses the importance of the religious constitution of humanity, acknowledging an inward and organic relationship between natural and divine.[16] In Christ God has let himself into the world in order to raise the entire world process—organically, culturally, socially—into a fullness in the divine.

THE SPIRITUALITY OF THE GERMAN CHARACTER

The German character, said Nevin, has a predisposition to religion. "Without a predisposition to religion, as a constituent element of his nature, man could never become religious at all. . . ."[17] The German does not rest easily in the external, temporal, and transient realms of human experience. The lives of Germans are of the soul, formed for love, friendship, poetry, and religion. The constitutions of some peoples have narrow and rigidly fixed organic restrictions, beyond which it is difficult to pass. The German is free and comprehensive, presumably available to the radical catholicity of the Incarnation. Nevin's appreciation for the German mind and spirit at times borders on adulation. One wonders what he would say of that mind and spirit from the perspective of one hundred years later. To Nevin the German can make himself at home in all foreign systems of thought, with the ability to understand or even to appropriate those systems to himself. The principle of vocational selection calls for the American Church to recognize this Germanic quality of openness, catholicity—with prejudice less firm than is common. "In the case of no emigration that could be brought to our shores, might it be expected that proper attention and cultivation would be so successful. . . . Ten German Papists may be made Protestant more easily than one from Ireland."[18]

Germans are highly literate, and many of the immigrants are educated. What is most sobering, of course, continued Nevin, is that these people have lost their hold on the distinctiveness of the Christian gospel. He observed infidelity and rationalism in the midst of a certain ignorance of religion. Many were "under the dominion of Popery"; yet they were not a "church-going" people and were obviously devoid of the hallowing associations of Protestant Sabbath. The mass emigrations of the nineteenth century led to the isolation of people in America, cutting them off from the good influence of the established order by barriers of language and thought. Why, wondered Nevin, did American Christians find it easier to evoke zeal and imagination for the missionary task in foreign lands than to the responsibilities in this nation? Americans simply ask, "Am I my brother's keeper?"

Meanwhile, of course, the Roman Church was making efforts to organize and consolidate the entire German emigration as an enclave within its own ecclesiastical order. The established Protestant congregations of German origin were incapable of meeting this challenge. They were too poor and had trouble taking care of themselves. The field was too extensive to be reached by the regular ministry. This was a task, said Nevin, for the Tract Society and the colporteur system: "Let the colporteur go forth among them with his books and tracts published in their own language. Let him converse with them kindly and plainly, endeavoring to remove their prejudices, correct their errors and win their hearts to Christ."[19] This was the system of Evangelical Christianity that was so successful in the sixteenth century, when tracts, treatises, and disputations were disseminated and defended among the people of an existent Roman Christianity.

THE CATHOLICITY OF MISSIONS

This argument for home missionary efforts is not representative of the best of Nevin's thought. It is undeveloped at some key levels, but it was written for the denominational newspaper. Many of its basic ideas have profound implications, as we have already seen, and must be understood in relation to the maturation of his thought as represented by the publication of *The Anxious Bench, The Mystical Presence,* the *Sermon on Church Unity,* and his essays "The Sect Spirit," "Catholicism," and "Early Christianity." There is little doubt that the Mercersburg years were to provide the occasion for the maturation of a theology that had only curious intimation during Nevin's time at Princeton and Western. The essay on the home missionary task, described in the *Weekly Messenger* of May 31, 1843, does not yet reveal the sophistication of Nevin's incarnational thought. But the allusions are there—especially in the notion of vocational selection. Missing, however, is the theology of regeneration discussed in chapter 4, in which conversion is understood not basically as the multiplication of individual souls but as a taking up of the living economy of the world into the wholeness of Christ. In the essay "Catholicism" (1851), Nevin wrote: "The imagination that the outward mission [to individuals] here may be carried through first, and inner mission left behind as a work for future leisure, is completely preposterous. . . . To make the reign of Christ more deep and inward for the life of the world, is at the same time to prepare the way correspondingly for its becoming more broad and wide."[20]

Nevin's theology is public and catholic. It is directed toward the widest common life of the world and is not confessional at all, in the usual sense of that word. As Linell Cady suggests in her book *Religion, Theology, and American Public Life,* "Public theology, eschewing the impossible ideal of universal intelligibility, will situate itself within a recognizable tradition. . . . [T]his inevitable situatedness does not legitimate confessional or authoritarian modes of reflection."[21] Cady calls for a reconfiguration of the public-private paradigm that has dominated American public life: "The most pressing need is to cultivate a sense of public life as not simply a collectivity of individuals with private ends but a genuine common life within which individuals share significant goals."[22] This is precisely the reconfiguration that distinguished Nevin's theology a century and a half ago, and has been discussed in previous chapters of this book. As we have seen, Nevin's idea of public and private appears in his distinction between catholicity as wholeness and as allness. And the concept of a common life that is more than a collectivity of individuals is present in his radical catholicity—thereby affecting his ideas of missiology and evangelism. As a matter of fact, he alters the sectarian and Evangelical tendency to transform eschatology into an imminent apocalyptic expectation of the millennium, associated with the ingathering of individual souls. The latter is an outward, external manifestation, according to Nevin; it expresses a mechanical view of salvation. In this understanding the great purpose of the gospel is rescuing the perishing, bringing them to heaven, helping souls in their separate individual character to flee from the wrath to come and secure a good hope against the day of judgment.[23] As Pierce Beaver has put it: *sound* eschatology found occasional expression in those like Jonathan Edwards who asserted that the terrible time of the Church's trials had passed and that the coming of latter-day glory awaited the inward response of the people. "On the one hand, the witness of the Church was by God's own design made prerequisite to the End; and, on the other, the individual's concern for the End was directed away from his own personal fate to the gathering of all peoples unto Christ."[24] Nevin would alter that interpretation further by asserting that the individual's personal fate is lifted up into a wholeness that is the proper force of the Incarnation. It is not so much a "gathering of *all* peoples" as a conversion of the universal depths of human art, philosophy, and science. Pure naked individuality was an abstraction for Nevin.

There is, in Nevin's thought, a gradual movement away from the discussion of the outward sense of mission and evangelism. Most likely this is because he became more and more concerned with the address of Christianity to the internal life of the society and culture. As he became more certain of the catholic nature of the Incarnation, he saw the individualism and the utilitarian salvationism of American religious life as a matter of grave concern. His own thought, directed toward the common life of humankind in America, became scholarly, inward, and catholic. The understanding of missions became less and less linked to the activism of America's voluntary societies. The concern was for America itself and for whether the Church, in its sectarian and individualistic form, was capable of maintaining the spiritual constitution of the nation. In its feverish activity on behalf of saving souls and assuring the moral integrity of individuals, the Church had neglected the inward regeneration of American culture. It had assumed, incorrectly, that dealing with people in an external and quantitative fashion would guarantee the world's salvation. "Religion degenerates with [the sect mind] into a trade," noted Nevin in 1849, "in which men come to terms with God on the subject of their salvation, and lay away their special acquisitions as a sort of outward property for convenient use."[25]

However, in Christ there is a new creation, not merely a mechanism for individual enlightenment or regeneration. God has already altered the course of history, of being itself. The Church as the Body of Christ exists as the mystical presence of the new creation in the world. Just as a deposit of leaven is the microcosm of the whole mass of meal, containing the full power of transformation; just as that same leaven requires an inward process to gain its potential end; so the Church is the mystical presence of the new creation.

> There is an inward *mission* . . . here, which grows as much necessity out of its relation to the world, as the mission it has to overshadow the whole world with its branches, and which it is urged too with just as much necessity . . . to carry forward and fulfill. The prayer, *Thy Kingdom Come,* has regard to the one object quite as much as the other. This comes by the depth of its entrance into the substance of humanity . . . as a process of intensification. . . .[26]

It was difficult for Americans to transcend the natural world. Nature beckons Americans to control it yet offers to provide in its abundance for all that they need think or do. Nature is ample; and Americans are convinced of the divine potential of what is natural. I interpret Nevin to suggest that we do not really understand what is natural. That is to say, there is an otherness to nature that leads to the supernatural. The question raised by Nevin is: Do we know what the natural is naturally? The issue is again very crucial in the world of late-twentieth-century scholarship in religion. As historians of religion investigate the realms of nonliterate cultures such as those of the Native Americans, they tend to deplore the use of "supernatural" as an intrusive form of Euro-American exploitation. However, the matter is not that simple.

BEYOND MISSIOLOGICAL NATURALISM

As Nevin put it, it is "rationalistic supernaturalism" that must be opposed. This latter begins as a genuine attempt to defend the faith against the powers

of modernity that threaten it. However, it holds true faith in bondage to a
rationalistic system of thought that fails to honor the mystery of the Incarnation. It is not conscious or open rationalism but a circumscribing of the supernatural under the assumption that it may be contained within rational systems
of beliefs.[27] Here again we find Nevin opposing the very confessionalism he
is accused by historians of representing. Rationalistic supernaturalism acts as
though its enterprise is more than linguistic. For Nevin, nature is known and
understood from the perspective of the whole in which it exists. His radical
catholicity saved him from rationalistic supernaturalism. What the supernatural
really refers to is the vision of the natural; it knows what is natural by seeing
the world of creature and constituent from the perspective of the new creation
in Christ—a cosmic Christ. The supernatural is an idea, of course, as is the
natural—its reality fashioned very distinctly in the affirmation and apprehension of a real grace meeting the person from beyond her own being, and not
in any inward persuasion or feeling simply of the person herself.

The wholeness of God and his creation, made mystically present in
Christ, is an appositional reality. It is known by virtue of the manner in which
it shares order and meaning with us in ordinary circumstances. The world
becomes natural not because we know it by investigation but because the
whole—the supernatural—gives us eyes to see. "Man," writes Loren Eiseley,
"is not totally compounded of the nature we profess to understand. Man is
always partly of the future." Doubt, said Eiseley, is "the power to make everything natural without the accompanying gift to see, beyond the natural, to
that inexpressible realm in which the words 'natural' and 'supernatural' cease
to have meaning."[28]

America, and the utilitarian Christianity that haunts its temples, tends to
honor the power to make everything natural without the accompanying gift
to see beyond. Henry Nash Smith, in his classic work *Virgin Land,* writes of
certain geographical theories that were used to support the notion of "the
westward course of empire." The point is, the westward course of empire was
more properly a religious idea than the political and economic motivations it
readily fostered. Smith explores the prominence of this idea in the geopolitical
thought of William Gilpin, friend of Andrew Jackson and later governor of
the Colorado Territory. Gilpin burned with an ecstatic vision of the succession
of empires in a "hereditary line of purpose" that culminated in the "Republican Empire of North America."

"Only by a heroic response to the challenge of universal history," writes
Smith, "can the nation fulfill its mission, which Gilpin describes in apocalyptic
language."[29] The very topography of North America was to be a factor in
shaping a new people who would live in harmony and union. In 1860, at the
threshold of the Civil War, Gilpin wrote with a note of desperation: "[T]he

holy question of our Union lies in the bosom of *nature* . . . , not in the trivial temporalities of political taxation, African slavery, local power, or the nostrum of orators however eminent."[30] Nature, as present to the frontier senses of Americans, was a benevolent reality that contained all that was essential to human salvation. It was the mission of America to be transformed by nature and to carry its message to the world.

In the sectarian mind of America, the missionary impulse was closely related, therefore, to the natural reality of this sacred place. That was so whether one spoke as a proponent of the national faith or in the pious tongue of revivalistic Evangelicalism. Nevin's public theology challenges this naturalistic assumption not simply on the basis of a positivism of revelation but from the perspective of the whole order of God. The whole of being may be present to us, but not in fullness. Accordingly, the meaning of life is not comprehended in the natural order of things; nor is the end to which we move a mere course from cradle to grave. "Opinion, speculation, dreamy sentiment . . . are not enough. . . . [K]nowledge must follow faith . . . the power of acknowledging the supernatural . . . the real presence of a new order of life, which is made to be actually at hand in the mystery of the Church."[31] It becomes increasingly clear that Nevin's understanding of the supernatural is linked to the idea of mystery itself. The natural is more than it seems to be, more than is measured or sensed. It points to and participates in the mystery beyond itself that is the supernatural. Nature and supernature coinhere; that is the truth of Incarnation.

Standing on the threshold of the Civil War, Nevin took issue with American nationalism. We had become, he said, "a world within ourselves," making "the order of supernatural grace one with the order of mere nature." The forces at work are compounded by a missionary impulse derived from a materialistic and quantitative understanding of the millennium. We have no perspective from which to comprehend the tremendous task before us—our mission to guide the internal conversion of our culture to the truth of the Incarnation. Our religion itself and our morality are shaped by utilitarian notions of profit and loss. Gain and godliness are run together in our minds.

In January 1861, in the midst of Southern secessionism and the attack on Fort Sumpter in South Carolina, John Nevin preached his sermon "Judgment and Duty" at the First Reformed Church in Lancaster, Pennsylvania:

> That the judgment of God which is upon us as a people at this time—full of present woe and fraught with the fear of greater woes to come—carries with it a reference to the general national sins . . . would seem to be plainly indicated by the form and manner of it as related to these sins themselves. It

is levelled and bent against them in the most direct way. What a rebuke of
our pride! What a commentary on our greatness! What an earthquake of
warming underneath our idolatrous worldliness, our unbelieving materialism,
our whole devotion to the interests of time and sense![32]

The judgment applies to American Christianity as it does to the political and
economic condition of the nation.

THE MISSION TO AMERICA: THE CHURCH OF THE CREED

The real mission of American Christianity is bound up with the restoration
of the Church as an essential element of faith itself. The Enlightenment rationalism and the rationalism of sectarian Christianity both deny the significance
of the Church as anything other than a voluntary association that may be
institutionally and functionally viable as a facilitator of the numeral extension
of Christianity. Rationalism is naturalistic. As an abstract system of thought, it
may simply assume that the present, natural world is the fullest reality, divine
as it may be. Sectarian rationalism, especially as it was expounded by Finney
and the revivalists, demands the address of the private individual to the truth
about private salvation that God has made available in the Bible. In both cases
the doctrine of the Church is not a matter of faith, as the Apostles' Creed
presents it. Even with all of its Christocentric utterances, American Christianity fails to understand the Incarnation. Outside this mystery, there is no comprehension of the natural world itself.[33]

The mystery of the Incarnation is not a fact that qualifies the natural
condition of the world in a kind of external supernatural way—a kind of
mechanical acting from outside and upon the world, so that people might do
honor to these powers. Rather, it is *present* as an objective constitution of
supernatural grace in a manner that is different from the natural world yet
makes the natural world redemptive. This "supernatural" reality lives *in* the
world of the natural and is celebrated in faith by the life of the Church, the
body of incarnational presence and awareness. The regeneration of life represented by the Church is not a matter of application of principles of psychology
or physiology; it is living in the mystical presence. Nevin rejects the notion
that the growth of naturalism is the potential *cause* of the loss of respect for
sacraments, Sabbath, Bible, and office of ministry. Instead, he sees the American Christian loss of faith in the Church as *cause for the rise of naturalism* and
the decline of imaginative faith for the vital living of these days. "Any argument for the supernatural, any plea for the Christological in its sound and

right form, to be of full force and effect in the end, must be at the same time ecclesiastical also, or, in other words, an argument for the old doctrine of the Church, as it stands enshrined in the early Creeds."[34]

There is little doubt that, as Nevin's thought matured, he gave less and less time to concern for the outward mission of Christianity. America had been attending feverishly to the duties of that mission both at home and abroad.[35] But the utilitarian Christianity of Bible and private judgment, of attention to the missionizing of *all* individuals in a conquest of the natural world order, was winning the day. Naturalism continued to gain as Christianity neglected its proper catholicity. Nevin grew weary of the mission to set the American Church on its proper course. It was a losing struggle, it seemed at times. As a matter of fact, Nevin's thought becomes less public toward the end of his life. Essays in the *Mercersburg Review* in 1877 included "The Testimony of Jesus," "The Spirit of Prophecy," and "Bible Anthropology." It is unfair to wrench these articles from the context of Nevin's whole life and its radical catholicity. Nevertheless, they do give the reader an impression that the great mind had settled in upon itself. The sounds of mission are muffled. The polemicist, critic, and public theologian is content to deal with biblical exposition and a kind of systematic introspection, sometimes homiletical and sentimental in tone.

The incarnational commitments are still there, but they do not engage the world in dialogue. "All that is comprehended in the ideas of creation, providence, and redemption, all the actualities of the world of nature, and all the realities of the mind or spirit, come together and stand together in Him [Christ] as a single constitution. . . . He is thus continually present and active in all the forms of outward material existence."[36] The material order, said Nevin, is sustained by the intentional word of God in Christ. We see the world properly, "not by outward sense, but by inward intellectual vision."[37] Here is a spiritual theology that may rival the best of this order of discourse. But it is not driven by the concern to convince the American churches of the necessity to do more than evangelize all the people of the world in this generation. Instead, as already stated, the ideas are set forth as spirituality. They move about the task of reconciling Old and New Testament, dealing with the distinctions between Jew and Christian, and developing a secure sense of the truth of Christian revelation. By this time Nevin accepts the fact that the common thinking in America is naturalistic—"as if the understanding could be the origin of its own light . . . any more than the will can be the origin of its own freedom or good!"[38] Naturalism is not interested in the missionary task of religion, except as in its subjective Evangelical form it directs itself to rescue the perishing. Gone is the critical rigor of 1851, when Nevin suggested that the most important and urgent task was the intensive mission to American life. The conversion of the dark continent of Africa could wait, he said then, but the radical catholic claim to all forms of American life could not.[39] By the time of Nevin's final retirement from the work at Franklin and Marshall College, it had become evident that American Christianity would not change, that it was satisfied with the Bible and private judgment, that it would not recognize the mystical presence of Christ in the Church and the world— except perhaps in God's own good eschatological time. In the present time, we lived at war with the powers of evil:

> [T]he battle of our salvation is to be fought out literally, and not in a meta-phorical sense merely [?], with the powers of darkness in the other world, and . . . the theatre of it lies mainly and essentially in that world, and not in the world of time and sense [the world of nature].[40]

eight

A TRANSCRIPT OF MYSTICAL PRESENCE: LITURGY AND THE AMERICAN CULTUS

In "Theology of the New Liturgy" John Nevin observed:

> As if the people, forsooth, could not find themselves properly in the Creed, the Te Deum, the Lord's Prayer, the Litany, the Ten Commandments, the Church Lessons and Collects, but only in the creations, extemporaneous or otherwise, let down upon them in the usual style from the modern pulpit. We have no such low opinion of the capacity of our laity. In the case before us, many of them at least have theological instincts, which are better and safer than all scholastic speculations; to say nothing of traditional beliefs, which no logic can set aside. To these instincts and beliefs we now make our confident appeal.[1]

The American people certainly have "theological instincts." They also have "traditional beliefs," of a sort. But if by tradition we mean the intellectual sense of continuity with a conserved body of teaching and practice associated with the history of Christianity, then we will question the wisdom of Nevin's assumptions in the preceding paragraph. He sought to appeal to the religious integrity of the people, assuming that the power of tradition and theological instinct was at work among them, guaranteeing their support of a refined historical liturgy. As late as 1867 Nevin was optimistic in this regard. He had not yet accepted the fact that the puritanical and pietistic cultus of American Christianity had advanced to the point where the American mind preferred "creations," especially "extemporaneous, . . . let down upon them in the usual style from the modern pulpit." Only Anglicanism, Eastern Orthodoxy, and (to some extent) Roman Catholicism have been able to sustain a ritual order of religion in which the people seem to find themselves properly in the drama of creed, Te Deum, lessons, collects, and litany. The great body of the

American people, whether in the context of churches or the wider public area, pride themselves in what they regard as unadorned simplicity and in words that are privately personal. We have not taken kindly to ritual, have perhaps not, therefore, understood the ritual patterns at work among us in the course of our ordinary existence.

In the liturgical renewal movements of the mid–twentieth century that have affected the worship life of mainstream traditions such as Presbyterian, Methodist, and United Church of Christ, the people have maintained a stoical toleration. They have continued to look at liturgical matters as, at best, adornments that preface the delivery of the sermon. In 1855, in semiretirement, Nevin wrote to Philip Schaff at Mercersburg, saying that he had "no heart, no faith, no proper courage" to continue working for a new liturgy. He had first become involved in the liturgical enterprise in 1849, when he was appointed chair of a committee of the synod, assigned to the task of examining various liturgies of the Reformed Churches and other works published on the subject. The committee was charged with evaluating forms that might be needed and was to "furnish specimens" appropriate to the Church in America.[2] The "general posture of the Church" made progress on this assignment very difficult to achieve, and Nevin resigned as chair in 1851. He continued to serve on the committee under Schaff's chairmanship.

The liturgical controversy was closely allied with the general unrest caused by the theological work of Nevin and Schaff in the development of the Mercersburg movement. There was a certain suspicion of anything coming out of Mercersburg. But, of course, the opposition justified itself from the standpoint of the general theological demeanor of American Protestantism, both clerical and lay. The incarnational thrust of Nevin's thought led him in the direction of liturgical theology. Already in his response to Finney's "new measures" and his formulation of a eucharistic theology in *The Mystical Presence,* Nevin had set a theological course that was informed by an unusual understanding (for his time) of the nature of ritual. Nevin's theology was public, but it was also catholic. He assumed that the theology he was formulating would make sense to America, that it could correct many of the false assumptions of a Protestantism that promised to lead the culture astray and end in its own ineffectiveness.

THE ANTIRITUAL DEVELOPMENT OF
THE AMERICAN CULTUS

A nation on the way to becoming a "city upon the hill" has little time to refine its ritual life. Yet Tom F. Driver, among others, has pointed out that "human beings, in all societies, everywhere and in all ages, have engaged in the making and performing of rituals."[3] America has not escaped this apparent ritual necessity among humans, as well as animals.[4] Presumably human beings have always found it essential to express some order and meaning for their existence by the use of certain gestural routines and patterns. Even the scientific enterprises of the modern world depend heavily on ritual. Ritual consists of an element of performance that takes place within a context of certain rules and schedules, which may be either fixed or movable. Ritual does not exist in an inferior relationship to the process of thinking or believing—or even to the sense of identity and belonging that are important to any society, sacred or secular. Ritual may exist prior to any concerted thought process or formulation of ideas or beliefs. It may make ideas "work" by accompanying them in human consciousness. Ritual is a fundamental and inescapable aspect of the human experience.

Americans have been nurtured to an antiritualistic bias that has been the result of Puritan assumptions and the spiritualistic impulses of the Continental Reformation. Puritanism championed an iconoclastic spiritualism that denied much significance to external or material modalities. The Puritans assumed that subjective and internal devotion was the essence of human religiousness and that objective realities were inconsequential or even satanic temptations. Pietism came to share some of the same assumptions. Certainly the Continental Reformers found themselves reacting to what they considered the excesses of Rome; and, in struggling to rid the Church of "magic" and "superstition," they left themselves open to the spiritualistic conclusions of reformers like Kaspar Schwenckfeld, who spoke of communion in the spirit and denied the necessity of elements like bread and wine in Christian worship. Martin Luther's own inclinations seemed at times to run counter to his attempt to retain the Mass and maintain it intellectually with his doctrine of consubstantiation.

Of course, the antiritualistic bias of much American thinking has not been shaped by Puritanism and Continental spiritualism alone. The Enlightenment religiousness that affected American thought in the late eighteenth and early nineteenth centuries was a powerful contributor to antiritualism. This thinking advocated a religious perspective that elevated a notion of autonomous human reason to the status of self-revelation. It was a form of religiousness that inherited the iconoclasm of Puritanism and the latitudinarian ideas of some Anglican thinkers. As Henry F. May has put it: "A generation of scholarship has shown us that the main citadels of New England Puritanism were the first to let in the Lockeian infiltrators. . . . During the Revolution, Nature's God and Jehovah were clearly on the same side if never quite the same person."[5] The Enlightenment in America, said May, "makes most sense when treated as religious history."[6] Although there may have been some ritual affectations and parodies employed by Enlightenment religionists, they stood basically in opposition to ritual as priestcraft and superstition. After all, nature itself was a kind of Scripture that yielded to private judgment in a direct and immediate way—quite similar to revivalistic Evangelicalism.

Perhaps not least of the sources of American antiritualism, of course, was the anti-Romanism characteristic of both the dominant Evangelical Protestant culture and the emergent Enlightenment thought. J. H. A. Bomberger, who in 1849 had recommended the appointment of a committee to begin work on a liturgy for the Reformed Church, apparently had little understanding of the true nature of liturgy. He had merely envisioned the collection of certain prayers and other pulpit aids to be used as models by the clergy in the conduct of worship. When the liturgy finally appeared, bearing the imprint of Nevin and Schaff, it encountered opposition by Bomberger and others who suspected it, as Luther Binkley has stated, "of Anglo-Catholic or Roman Catholic tendencies." In Binkley's words, Bomberger "contended for a subjectivistic liturgy rather than an objective liturgy." He wanted nothing to do with an "altar liturgy" or "priest's book."[7] Obviously, Bomberger's thought, like that of most of the opposition in the Reformed Church, was antiritualistic. It did not seek a liturgy at all, inasmuch as a liturgy is by nature not "subjectivistic" but ritualistic—an objective historical text for common prayer and action.

What becomes paradoxically apparent, therefore, is that we have been a people who engage in ritual even as we deny its reality, on both pietistic and rationalistic grounds. Nevin's efforts as a theologian were constantly at work in a public arena that was not especially hospitable to his ministrations. For Nevin, an authentic understanding of the Christian revelation required an altar liturgy, the common prayer of the historic catholic church centered in the eucharistic expression of the mystical union between Christ and the world.

Of course, much of the antiritualism encountered by Nevin and the Mercersburg movement was the result of an ineffective understanding of history, itself partly the result of the frontier circumstances of American society. Jon Butler has told of the laxity of Christian practice among seventeenth-century colonists.[8] However that may be true of the habits of people in New England and Virginia, it must be pointed out that one of the reasons for this deficiency among the German settlers of Pennsylvania had been the lack of resources and leadership. Many of the early immigrants were under the influence of the Pietism that had begun to affect Lutheran and Reformed churches in Europe. These people brought with them devotional books, Johann Arndt's *True Christianity,* some sermon books, and hymnbooks. As H. M. J. Klein put it in his *History of the Eastern Synod of the Reformed Church in the United States:* "There was not much interest shown for building churches or purchasing land for such buildings."[9] The first pastor to arrive (in 1710) was a Swiss Pietist named Samuel Guldin, who frequently preached to the people in houses, barns, or groves. But Guldin was not much interested in organization, only in the piety of people's lives. It remained for John Philip Boehm, a schoolmaster and layman, to attempt some kind of "Kirchen ordnung."

The unchurchly sentiment of much Pietism found a ready home in America, where there were no established traditions and the landscape had not yet been sacralized by Christian myth and symbol. This sentiment combined with the lack of resources and ordained clergy to fashion a religious life distinct, though not absolutely divorced, from the European setting. Charles Glatfelter, in his study of the early religious history of Pennsylvania, notes that about 90 percent of the Germans and Swiss were Lutheran or Reformed who were accustomed to a ministry of word and sacrament. "Unfortunately for them, their European traditions of a learned clergy functioning in an established church made it much more difficult to secure this ministry than it was for the Mennonites and other sect people."[10] Without adequate resources, the Reformed people of eastern Pennsylvania developed a style of Christianity that was democratic and pietistic, emphasizing those devotional ideas and attitudes that were later to find common cause with the development of revivalism and utilitarian salvationism. John Philip Boehm (in the eighteenth century) had sought to establish some order to this process by suggesting to the ecclesiastical authorities of the Reformed Church in Holland that they send enough "Palatinative Church Orders" for all of the fledgling congregations in America. However, the number of these church orders was so small that each minister was left to his own resources until well into the nineteenth century, when the committee to prepare a liturgy was formed in 1849.[11]

We may observe, therefore, that the pattern of religious life in America had developed in an antiritualistic and nonliturgical manner both by intent and as a result of the pragmatic circumstances of frontier democracy. Democracy, left to its own devices, is remarkably utilitarian and leveling.

When Nevin turned to the task of vindicating the liturgy produced in 1857 and revised in 1866, he proceeded to articulate the principles of the Mercersburg Theology, so ably set forth during the previous quarter century. The opposition accused the new liturgy of being ritualistic, of making too much of sacraments and too little of the Bible.[12] Nevin immediately issued his *Vindication of the Revised Liturgy*, and the *Mercersburg Review* for the same year published a lengthy version of "Theology of the New Liturgy."[13] Already in 1849, in reporting on the Baltimore Synod's action in appointing a liturgical committee, he had prophesied the coming controversy: "No liturgy," he wrote, "can go far beyond the reigning idea of worship."[14] Indeed, the reigning idea of worship was virtually to be identified with the utilitarian individualism of American revivalism. If the Church cannot understand the theological necessity of liturgy, said Nevin, then it will dabble in "forms," and the efforts to publish a liturgy will have been misplaced. "The conception of a liturgy in the true sense, as compared with our reigning unliturgical and *free* worship, is the conception of a real emancipation into the liberty of the children of God."[15]

LITURGY AND NATURE

Nevin's theology of liturgy is grounded in an understanding of nature itself. Liturgy provides the perception by means of which we may understand the longing to which nature points. Nature is to be understood from the perspective of the Incarnation of Christ's life and work. Nature's expectations are fulfilled and reconciled in Christ. "Nature," said Nevin, "is a divine liturgy throughout." One of the most beautiful portions of Nevin's prose appears at the end of the short essay "The Liturgical Movement" of 1849:

> The life of heaven, still more, is a liturgy, "like the sound of many waters," of the most magnificent and sublime order. What we need, in our present movement, is the full sense of what worship means in this view; sympathy with the music of the spheres, and with the song of the angels; the same mind that led the early church into the universal use of liturgies, without opposition or contradiction, so far as history shows, from any quarter.[16]

There is in nature the foretaste of heaven, nature and supernature not being "two different systems."[17] Liturgy is an act of ascesis that brings together the life of nature and the life of heaven. The Incarnation makes this liturgical, ritual reality possible. In Christ is *life,* the light that creates the world and asserts itself in the darkness. People are brought to God, said Nevin, "not by doctrine or example, but only by being made to participate in the divine nature itself" as that is embodied in Christ.[18] Humanity thus becomes "the Shechinah of glory."[19]

In his remarkable essay "The Church Year," he had already laid a foundation for liturgy in nature. Among all peoples it was possible to recognize a close relation of spiritual life to the constitutions of nature. In the human person the two realms were joined in consciousness. There is established a correspondence between inward and outward through the relationship between nature and human spirit. The sacred year is evidence of nature being invested with the religious significance to which it points. In the sacred year is expressed the reality of the life of humankind starting in nature and completing itself in religion. "Where the year is made to assume a sacred or religious form, by having the ideas of religion *lodged in its natural revolution,* we are not to conceive of the relation as being simply outward and artificial; but are bound to see in it rather a real connection between the things that are thus brought together."[20]

The sacred year creates time because it exists for the world as a whole. A political year is an arrangement of events in an artificial manner, conducive to the functioning of a nation. But the sacred year reflects the consciousness of nature itself as universal, and as invested with a reality that points beyond itself. The sacred year reminds us that human destiny is related to nature, which includes "a certain inward correspondence with the order and course of . . . supernatural facts, as well as with the spiritual economy itself which they underlie."[21] The sacred year, therefore, symbolizes and ritualizes the power of nature to show forth "the completion of a full circle in the process of all earthly life."[22] Festival days, says Nevin, enable a continual celebration of the "true and proper relationship of the two economies of nature and grace." They elevate us above the common level of the quotidian. This elevation is an ascesis, a withdrawal to the boundaries and beyond the boundaries where we are provided with a proper perception of reality. In other words, we withdraw from among the trees in order to see the forest.

In the pagan religious year, the visible creation bears traces of its divine origin, so that humans are conscious of the mysterious powers resident in nature. However, the perception of the mystery is without a transforming element, objective in character, enabling humans to discriminate "between the sign and the thing signified." The result is a perception of nature as turned in upon itself, invested with the fullness of divinity. Whether this paganism is rudimentary and superstitious or refined as in Greek and Roman naturalism, it is not without merit. It acts as a testimony and argument for the truth, showing what the religious constitution of humanity universally needs and seeks.[23]

There is in the pagan religious mind an idea of redemption, reflecting the sense that powers of darkness and evil press in upon humans, as, for example, they seem to do in the threatening days of the winter solstice. Hope and new birth, and a redemptive rising from death, are mirrored in the solar year. "To be real, this process must begin in the soul, must be spiritual."[24] The natural year, by itself, according to Nevin, has no power to see beyond itself, to perceive the supernature in nature, through whose significance it is "possible

for the symbolized idea to become fact. That requires the historical interven-
tion of a higher life. . . ."[25] It requires the discovery of the personal element
in nature itself and its redemptive suffering.

Nevin moves to a discussion of the Jewish year, of vastly higher order
than the pagan. In a sense, the Jews introduce history into nature. The divine
law invests nature with historical significance and introduces the Sabbath as
the center from which to view the completely physical time present in the
rest of the week. Nature is not set aside—it is still a manifestation of divine
power—but there is no absolute identification of divinity and nature. Nature
becomes a symbol of the Creator, calling into consciousness the actions of
human behavior and representing "God's actual dealings of grace with men."[26]

With the coming of Christ, the significance and power of nature and
humanity are fully revealed.

> The process of redemption is found moving its course, first in his person, in
> order that it may break forth in the full victory of Easter as a fact accom
> plished for the world at large. The religious year is redeemed, its mystery
> given its proper meaning. Nature appears transfused throughout with spirit
> and life. Grace reigns triumphant over all the months and seasons.[27]

The church year makes true ritual possible because religion in the form
of nature and religion in the form of history are integrated. The constitution
of the world (nature and history) is raised to a constitution of grace, the realm
of Incarnation. Humankind is now provided with the occasion of true worship, a liminal action that contemplates the life of the world. Liturgy celebrates
what has taken place; liturgy is the coming together of those whose lives are
constituted by the constitution of grace. Liturgy is bound up with the church
year: "[N]o method of Christian worship can ever be so effective for Church
purposes, as that which is based on the proper use of the ecclesiastical year.
. . . There is a most intimate connection between the use of such a scheme
of worship and the practical apprehension of the great facts of Christianity in
their proper form."[28] Liturgy and the church year are expressive of the heart
of Christianity.

Neglect of the system of liturgy and the church year moves the interests
of religion in the direction of Gnosticism or rationalism. The system keeps
the Christian life grounded in history. In America, where there has been increasing neglect of the system, we have witnessed a deterioration of Christianity into mere utilitarian salvationism and history-less sectarianism. Where the
system is ignored, said Nevin, "There can be no right sense of the Church,
no proper faith in the holy sacraments, no sound liturgical feeling, no active

sympathy with the grand facts which are set forth in the Creed, no firm hold on *the abiding power* of these facts, as an order of grace moving onward in *sublime correspondence with the order of nature* to the end of time."[29]

Nevin's theology of the liturgy is an explanation of those "great facts of Christianity" that are the correspondent consummation of the mystery of creation to which nature bears witness. Much of the opposition to the new liturgy produced by the committee influenced by Nevin and Schaff was directed at its elite character. The adversaries protested that only educated people, not plain folk, would profit from these beautiful services.[30] Nevin disagreed, but, as suggested previously, he was probably wrong in his assessment of the American mind. "The new liturgy was scriptural, historical, artistic, and Evangelical Catholic," writes Binkley.[31] These were all characteristics that Nevin had hoped would emerge as Americans took stock of their culture and resisted the utilitarian individualism that was fashioning our religion and our politics. He assumed that sectarianism and the old rationalism writ large could not win the day if Americans were presented with the artistic, historical, and catholic truth of Christianity.

WHAT IS EVANGELICAL THEOLOGY?

The opposition questioned the Evangelical soundness of the liturgy, but it is *their* views that are not Evangelical, said Nevin. In fact, the views of the adversaries are heretical. Of course, what was difficult for Nevin to comprehend was that any discussion of heresy in the modern world is difficult to sustain. It ends up being done either on a rarefied theological level that bypasses the leveling minds of democratic folk or from what seems to be a sectarian or confessional perspective that is contrary to the radical catholicity and historical foundations of Nevin's own thought. What does the average American care about Te Deum, litany, lessons and collects, and creed? Even if it be true, as Nevin assumed, that the people could possibly find themselves properly in these symbolic realities, they are not likely to be interested in the experiment. They already are possessed by a set of religious assumptions nurtured by Puritanism, Wesleyanism, Pietism, and the pragmatic subjectivism of a frontier mentality. "Evangelical" does not mean what purveyors of the anxious bench maintain, says Nevin. But who will listen? Not the large numbers of Americans for whom the "evangel" is an excited claim to possess an experience that one renews from time to time, accompanied by a show of outward virtue. "Simon Magus," wrote Nevin, "dreamed of purchasing the gift of God, and clothing himself with it in the way of outward possession. *He* was a quack; the prototype and prince of evangelical quacks." [32]

In John Nevin's thought the full sense of the evangel centers on the Incarnation. It is not only a kerygma or a proclamation but a new creation— something has happened in the perception of the world, something that has to do with the destiny of humankind *in* the world. A new creation is hardly a possession to be claimed by individuals eager to be assured of their religious expectation. Rather, it is a new *constitution,* as Nevin had maintained repeatedly. For him it was a new and divine consciousness that shares itself with us, a mystery in which we continue to grow sacramentally.

THE CHRISTOCENTRISM OF THEOLOGY

To be Evangelical is to be appreciatively aware of the new creation, as the Church has been from the earliest times. Evangelical theology will therefore be Christocentric, creedal, and objective-historical, "involving thus the idea of the Church as a perennial article of faith." [33] Evangelical theology is catholic because "the mystery of the incarnation involves in itself . . . a new order of existence for the world which is as universal in its own nature as the idea of humanity." [34] As has been observed repeatedly, the wholeness in question is not to be confused with the numerical *all* of humankind, nor even with an elect or select number of that abstract aggregate. Much of American Evangelicalism (and also Universalism) errs at precisely this issue, said Nevin. Of course, even Calvin had allowed his thought to be distracted by this error in judgment. In all these cases, Evangelical activity is directed toward an obsession with numbers, with the salvation and conversion of individuals. Are *all* saved? Are *some* saved? How shall we direct our energies? These are questions aroused by a failure to understand that God was in Christ reconciling the world to himself. This means that individuality and the "parts" of the world come into view as the product of the wholeness of the new creation. They are not the factoral elements making up the whole.

This is Christocentric thinking, as opposed to the rationalistic and naturalistic thinking of American Evangelicalism. "The *whole* fact of Christianity gathers itself up fundamentally into the single person of Christ." [35] For Nevin, the center of the world and of our thinking is a tremendously important fact. In understanding this, he seems to anticipate the insights of twentieth-century historians of religion and writers of spirituality who call attention to the significance of the center in both Weltanschauung and religious consciousness.

Much Christian theology vacillates and plays between the poles of anthropo-
centric divinity and simple theocentric divinity, wrote Nevin.[36] Such religious
systems as these have had their place in the development of religion; versions
of them have intermarried with Christian teaching. However, the first principle of Christian life and thought is the Person of Christ. Christ is in the
world, thereby providing us with the perspective of his mystical presence in
our ethics, our historical sense, and our knowledge of and relation to God.[37]

IN THE BOSOM OF THE CREED

The Evangelical Catholic theology of the new liturgy "moves in the bosom
of the old Creeds, the original regula fidei of the Christian world."[38] The
Apostles' Creed was recognized by the fifth and sixth centuries as the common
rule of faith, which the Church catholic had held from its beginnings in apostolic authority. "The symbol," said Nevin, "has been received through all ages
as the primary and most fundamental expression of the Christian faith."[39] The
symbol, as he called the creed, is fundamental and lies at the foundation of
Evangelical unity. As a symbol, it is the bearer of power and meaning beyond
the ability of the mind to give it full explanation. Accordingly, the creed is
not like a confession as a summary of doctrine, but it is a symbol to be
apprehended in faith, for what it sets before us of the incarnate reality of the
gospel. One might say, in Nevin's understanding, that the creed is "a direct
transcript . . . of what the Gospel is to the contemplation . . . turned wholly
upon the Person of Christ. Such faith is necessarily ruled by its object; the
Creed, in other words, . . . must unfold itself . . . in the order of . . . the
fundamental facts . . . growing forth from the mystery of the Incarnation."[40]
The creed is the method for the apprehension of the gospel and dare not be
set aside. The objective character and movement of the creed has been denied
by American Christianity under the influence of Puritanism, Methodism, and
the salvationism of new measures revivalism.[41] Through the symbolic power
of the creed, all doctrine is Christologically shaped.

THEOLOGY AS OBJECTIVE-HISTORICAL

It should be obvious from the Christocentric and creedal characteristics of the
theology of the new liturgy that the theology is not a set of subjective notions
but an apprehension of the supernatural as it is joined to the natural history
of the world. The theology is objective and historical, not bound into the

subjectivism of the American notions of Bible and private judgment. The theological sense of revelation preserves the character and role of the objective and historical in relation to the knowledge and experience of God. The Christian understanding proceeds from the manifestation of the supernatural as the proper order of the natural. Revelation is the discovery that the meaning of the world and of nature cannot be understood on their own terms. As Nevin wrote,

> Universally, it would seem, the inward illumination is bound to the outward manifestation. God does not speak to the souls of men immediately and abruptly, as enthusiasts and fanatics fondly dream. . . . The order of all true supernatural teaching is, the objective first, and the subjective or experimental afterwards, as something brought to pass only by its means.[42]

Salvation is therefore not in the individual experience or faith but in the mystery of the Incarnation, which is objective, historical, and interpersonal. The subjective, turned in upon its private conversion, is "at best only a spurious evangelicalism . . . more nearly allied to the flesh than to God's Spirit."[43]

THE SACRAMENTAL CHURCH

The new order of existence constituted for the world by the fact of Incarnation is not, then, a mere memory or a subjective appropriation but a matter of perennial reality. The gospel is "once for all" in the sense that once having entered the life of the world, it is part of its historical being to the end of time. The world is now invested with "a supernatural economy" made constantly visible by the Holy Catholic Church in its sacramental representation of the mystical union of Christ and the world.[44] The objective and historical character of the Incarnation means that it is not to be lost under some vague notion of things spiritual, not even as the work entirely of the Holy Spirit. The Church, the creed reminds us, is a necessary postulate of faith. The Church is a symbolic reality, therefore objective and historical—a mystery to contemplate and to manifest.

To reinterpret Nevin: we do not believe in the Church because we are convinced of the superior qualities and attributes of the empirical institution. We contemplate the Church, respond to it in faith, because it proceeds from Christ. Faith, in this sense, is like the trustful response we give to one we love. Faith is elicited from us by the power of the symbolic reality. It is simultaneously deliberate and spontaneous. Our wills are directed to the symbolic reality in order that we may understand life by means of the Church. The

Church, therefore, is more than it seems to be in its empirical form; yet it is most definitely historical and objective. It points beyond itself, yet it presents to the world the mystical sense of the world's own basic meaning and order, as that has been effected by the Incarnation.[45]

"In this sense, most assuredly, salvation is of the Church, and not of the world; and to look for it in the world, by private spiritualistic negotiations . . . is to look for it where it is not to be found."[46] For Nevin this theological understanding made more of Christ, and was more Evangelical, than unchurchly theologies based on subjective experience and biblical rationalism.

The Church, then, is a sacramental reality that shares its sacraments with the world. The sacraments are not mere outward signs but "seals . . . of the actual realities themselves . . . mysteries in which the visible and the invisible are bound together. . . ."[47] Sacraments are elements of the natural order that communicate their own potential by investment with the supernatural. Supernature and nature are one in the mystical union of Christ and his Church in the world. The sacraments manifest this union, the Eucharist being the central act by which the mystical presence is manifest. "A theology," wrote Nevin, "which is truly Christocentric, must follow the Creed, must be objective, must be historical, . . . must be churchly, . . . must be sacramental *and liturgical*."[48] In other words, truly Evangelical theology requires liturgical expression of the affinities discussed in this chapter. "It can never be satisfied with anything less than an altar liturgy." Enemies of the liturgy are apostates, un-Evangelical, said Nevin. They reflect the sectarian generations of American religion, with its abstract individualism and naive subjectivism.

Opponents of the liturgy tend to use worship, continued Nevin, even when they accept "liturgical" forms, as incidental to the experiences, commitments, and ideas of assembled individuals. Baptism, for example, transmits nothing in and of itself. It merely affirms the intent of what has been experienced or decided. Christianity is then purely subjective, centered in the human mind, with no account made of objective mediation of grace. Of course, the opponents of liturgy pretend to center their experience upon "Christ and Him crucified." But do they confess that " 'Jesus Christ is come in the flesh,' not in appearance only, and not for a season only, but in full reality, and *for all time*"?[49] For them the supernatural remains outside the natural, except as it is resolved into a spiritual presence, reaching into the minds of humans directly from heaven. Even justification by grace through faith, in this perspective is not tied to anything objective and continuingly historical but resides simply in the subjective assurance a person may have of God's mercy in his own mind, "becoming thus, in fact, justification by fancy or feeling."[50] Sacraments then become mere signs of grace absent, not seals of grace present.

A TRANSCRIPT OF SACRIFICIAL GRACE

The conflict between those who oppose the liturgy and those who are its proponents is a conflict of theological systems, said Nevin, not merely a controversy over forms and responses. It is a conflict between those who claim to be Evangelical but are merely subjective spiritualists, and those who recognize the presence of the Incarnation in Church, creed, and sacraments, objectively and historically considered. To use Nevin's own metaphor, the liturgy is "a transcript" of the mystical presence of the Incarnation. It is a text of words and actions that communicate the reality of the Word made flesh.[51] In the Eucharist, for example, the truth of the gospel is "concentrated into a single, visible transaction, by which it is made as it were transparent to the senses, and caused to pass before us in immediate living representation."[52] As B. A. Gerrish has put it: "By 'sacrament' Nevin means the total liturgical event as an operation of the Spirit *through* appointed means."[53] Everything must be taken together. The liturgical event gives objective, historical witness; it provides continuing evidence of the mystical presence. It delivers the Lord's Supper, *transcribes* it, so that, as Gerrish writes (interpreting Nevin again), *in* the Supper, "we communicate with the living Savior himself in the fullness of his glorified person, and we are made to participate in his true and proper life. Indeed, we partake of his 'substance.' The participation is real, substantial, and essential."[54] The virtue of it is not the *product* of faith. Faith is elicited by the grace actually present. This, of course, as pointed out earlier, does not mean a crass and literal mastication. The presence is objective, but it is greater than, more than, the local or merely "natural" formations many seem to claim in reductionist fashion.

Here is an interesting understanding of both liturgy and ritual. The individual is not merely a believer who works out a form of private salvation that spends a lifetime trying to keep her holy after her conversion. Rather, the individual is not complete in himself or herself. The self always exists *in Christ*. In Christ we are new creatures in a new creation. For the self to be in Christ, it must live in appositional receptivity to that "single visible transaction" whereby Christ is eaten, received substantially. In Nevin's thought we must not forget that Christ's life was a sacrifice. It was in some sense an offering up of humanity to the love and justice of God. "Under all systems of worship," wrote Nevin, "religion has ever been made to centre in the altar and the offering of sacrifice; while, by partaking of what was thus offered, the worshipper was supposed to come into the nearest communion with the object of his worship."[55] The ritual action was an essential, objective circumstance, removing the natural self from the boundaries of its ordinary presumption.

Sacrifice is a ritual action in which the self recognizes its communal reality in relation to God, who accepts and transcends the presumptions of the natural self. Therefore, the central ritual activity by means of which we live in the new creation is one in which sacrifice is enacted in its fullness. More is involved than some general communion with God, or some mechanical transaction between the individual and God. There is "the necessity of a true, living conjunction with the sacrifice itself. The lamb whose life was poured out as an offering for sin, must be itself incorporated as it were with the life of the worshipper, to give him a fair and full claim on the value of its vicarious death. It became to him an atonement, by entering really into his person."[56]

Christ is in us, but he is not contained; we are contained in his body, our selfhood the expression of the new creation. "The believer always feels that the power of which he is thus possessed is not from himself. . . . [I]t is not *he* that works, but Christ lives and works in him."[57] The destruction of the old and also the creation of the new, in the process of redemption, are alike Christ's work. Ritual is a form of human knowledge, of *knowing*. It is not action that is taken to demonstrate or act out what one knows. It is a recognition that we are always more than we know. In ritual we *know* that this is so. The reality known is not to be found in the outward sign alone, nor in the inward experience, but in a relation between the two that is expressed in response to the self-giving of the other. That is what is known as grace. The liturgy is a transcription of the whole ritual action, communicating the reality of the new creation as

> a moment in time and of time
> a moment not out of time, but in time, in what we call history:
> transecting, bisecting the world of time, a moment in time
> but not like a moment of time,
> a moment in time but time was made through that moment:
> for without the meaning there is no time, and that moment
> of time gave the meaning.[58]

The liturgy transcribes the importance of partaking of the sacrifice. It transcribes the sacrifice itself and lives through the eating and drinking.

BEYOND FAITH AS TRANSACTION

Those who opposed the liturgy in Nevin's time were guilty of separating the outward and inward aspects of the ritual action. Even the renowned German theologian Isaac Dorner betrayed the Evangelical Catholic nature of liturgy by accusing Nevin of saying nothing about "faith." Faith, wrote Dorner, is the Evangelical reality that responds in conversion to the true knowledge of Christ. Nevin, according to Dorner, puts Christ "immediately into front view as a primordial and central truth."[59] This means that, for Dorner, Nevin's thought takes an ancient, "in part anti-Reformation position. . . . The telescope of Christian inquiry, with him, has not the Christology for its *object,* in order to find in it the centre of the whole; it is made to be the presupposition, one knows not how reached, for the Christian thinking itself."[60]

What Dorner failed to recognize in Nevin's theology was that faith moves through the mystery of the Incarnation. Faith is itself *evidence* of the new creation in Christ. This new creation is an objective constitution in the New World that must be comprehended in faith. It can be comprehended in no other way, inasmuch as it is not the object of philosophical speculation but the contemplation of an other that is, indeed, what Dorner denied—"the great primordial centre from which all has been evolved."[61] Nevin's thought does not shut out the significance of faith. But faith is not for Nevin some subjective act of affirmation. Faith is the manner in which we take our position in the center from which all flows.[62] Otherwise, faith is in danger of becoming simple human subjectivity. Nevin supposes that he and Dorner are not really so far apart as the American opponents of the liturgy would have them be. The latter were in search of a champion and assumed they had found it in Dorner. However, they tended to understand Dorner in the Anabaptist supernatural rationalistic and common "Methodistical" sense of much American Christianity.

For John Nevin the American Evangelical sect system was in danger of setting up an abstract and subjective spiritualism, the nature of which Dorner did not appear to understand "sitting away off in Berlin."[63] Dorner was tolerant of American Evangelicals because he assumed that they preached Christ and emphasized the Atonement, whereas Nevin's emphasis on the Incarnation was to Dorner evidence of disregard for the *inward,* for a transactional faith in the Atonement.[64] This led Dorner to be suspicious of the liturgy as sacerdotal, neglecting the sacrificial significance of Christ's suffering and death. Of course, this characterization of the liturgy was misplaced. Nevin rightfully called attention to the fact that the liturgy was "baptized" in the atoning sacrifice, "bathed in it one may say, from beginning to end."[65] It was, after all, an altar liturgy, and it is pulpit liturgies that are by their "very nature at once unsacrificial and unsacramental."[66] In Nevin's understanding, the liturgy is a transcription of the Incarnation in the life of the Church, bringing inward and outward, subject and object, into a new relationship centered in Christ. It carries along "the lively sense of the great Christian facts, in the bosom of which only the ideas of atonement and justification can be kept from evaporating finally into sheer rationalistic dreams."[67]

Dorner did not understand the liturgy because his own theology veered too far from the historical reality of the Incarnation in Church and world. Dorner, said Nevin, diverged from the Christological center as it was set forth in the Apostles' Creed. Dorner accused the liturgy of being too expressive of the mystical spirit of the Eastern Church. Nevin accepted this accusation, defending the liturgy as more than a "mechanical echo of the cultus of the sixteenth century,"[68] as reaching for the catholicity present in the liturgical spirit of the early Church as it has been manifest in the ongoing mystical presence of Christ in Eucharist and Church. Dorner had placed his own trust in the possible resuscitation of the dead Protestantism of Germany. His sympathies lay in captivity to a Protestant rejection of the catholicity expressed by the Catholicism that was present before the Reformation. He rejected any notion of sacramentality that extended beyond some meager deference to the Lord's Supper. For example, he did not understand the ministry as that office which "holds immediately and directly from Christ Himself."[69] Sound Protestantism, for Dorner, required a repudiation of sacramental, hierarchical, and "magical" conceptions of ministry.

Dorner, like most opponents (real or imagined) of Mercersburg Theology and its liturgy, denied the dialectic of nature and supernature in the historical constitution of the Christian Church. From the perspective of the late twentieth century, it might be said that Dorner and his American compatriots had created a new religion out of the residue of the sixteenth-century Reformation. Their orientation in subjective faith had little sense of objective historical continuity, even though they may have sought to affirm some agreement with certain individuals among the representatives of the early Church, and with selected parts of subsequent Church history. Their opposition to the liturgy was evidence of their departure from the radical catholicity of the Church. It offered demonstration of their inability to comprehend the manifest reality and mystical presence of the Incarnation in its fullness. They lived in opposition to the idea of the Church as it stands in creed. They did not understand, therefore, the objective character of the liturgy as a transcription of the constitution of grace in which the response of faith resides. Nevin wrote:

> Against all this I maintain that the authority of Christ's presence and person (objective Christianity exhibited to us in Christ) is the ground of all subjective Christianity. Faith, in its last and deepest sense, is simply submission (free, but yet unseeing also, and *implicit*) to such objective authority. . . . The Christianity which was originally in Christ, must be for the Christian

world an objective authority till the end of time. . . . In some way the general life of Christianity (which is the Church) must come between all individual faith and the letter of Scripture. . . . If Germany, in the person of Professor Dorner (even though he should be commended to us by an angel from heaven itself), came preaching to us now *what is after all another Gospel,* born of the general confessional demoralization which seems to be sweeping all theology there into the maelstrom of *humanitarianism*—Germany, in this case, will preach to us in vain.[70]

Not so, Professor Nevin. Angels, or messengers of some sort, have commended this religious message to America. And America has responded enthusiastically, bringing to life many forms of the "humanitarianism" you foresaw as a maelstrom. I think John Nevin knew this was happening; however, he had little choice but to employ his theological insights in dialogue with the public discourse of the emergent American religion and culture.

CONCLUSION

It was evident by the time of Nevin's death in 1886 that the American nation was well on its way to the shaping of a national and a religious life that had substantially ignored his critical assessments. By the end of the nineteenth century a form of American nationalism was employed in the justification of conquest. Religious pluralism was developing a kind of cosmopolitanism that ignored Nevin's radical catholicity in favor of naturalistic idealism. The metaphors of Christian doctrine were used in support of private judgment and social perfectionism.

It would seem that Nevin was aware of the failure of his understanding of a new creation that would call the Church and the nation into judgment, even as it manifested itself in the development of the American people. His disappointment, however, did not send him into spiritualistic retreat from the public domain in which all theology must be done. After all, he had consistently called attention to the principle of development, which rejected no phase in the history of Christianity. He had insisted on the relevance of Saint Matthew's record of Christ's commission, with its assurance of "Lo, I am with you always, even to the end of the world." The new creation, once present, does not disappear from history. The question is: By what vision do we recognize and celebrate its presence, when the Church becomes a fragmented plurality of naturalistic claims based on notions of private judgment and subjective experience? Presumably, that is the question Nevin could not answer in his latter days.

The life of John Williamson Nevin is descriptive of the struggle of American religious thought to find itself. Cushing Strout writes: "One of the extraordinary things about American literature is how late it came to be regarded as a national tradition."[1] In the case of religious thought, Jonathan Edwards had struck a blow for independence and the development of an American theology already in the eighteenth century. And there was a steady flow of this Americanistic thought through to Nathaniel Taylor and Horace Bushnell. Even Emerson shared in the flowering. Yet the confessionalism that accompanied much of the reaction to the Americanization of Christianity tended to model itself along the lines of European theology with its devoted attention to system. Nevin's theology holds the wisdom of Continental theology in dialectical tension with the religious experience of the emergent American Republic. His theological style is not governed by the same devotion to Protestant scholasticism as is the work of his old mentor, Charles Hodge. However, it maintains a traditional prophetic edge in relation to the more naturalistic assumptions of Horace Bushnell.

John Nevin is an American theologian. He is a prevenient postmodern thinker. He tends to reject structures of thought that seek to control the subject under investigation, thereby forcing the subject into objective status. There is the sense that we are addressed by an "other" in our thinking, that this other is not reducible to our standards of measurement or to the signification we may be impelled to give it (him, her). Nevin's understanding of the Heidelberg Catechism is characterized by this loyalty to the symbolic power of language and form, a loyalty that distinguishes the catechism from confessions as repository of truth. His thought is both evocative and systematic, but, as I have shown, Nevin's sense of system is that of thorough and critical encounter with the subject. He does not do systematic theology in the manner of system building. Instead, his systematic thought is the result of his response to the circumstances of public life, which reflects the natural religious order as it awaits the illuminating activity of the new creation in Christ. System becomes the intensive critical interpretation of the Incarnation, addressed to the world and embodied in the life of the Church. System articulates the intellectual means whereby the inner life of humanity is raised in response to the external movement of public historical events.

Nevin is an American theologian, therefore, in the manner in which his systematic thought is addressed to the public agenda. There is a public character to his theology because the new creation is a public reality. The mystical union of divine and human celebrated in the Eucharist is a worldly and dynamic proceeding. For John Nevin the Incarnation represents a radical and realized catholicity. It is realized because it is present in the world, radical insofar as it rejects all realized claims to the fullness of the truth of God in Christ. Nevin develops the notion of catholicity as wholeness in response to the American inclination to think of catholicity as allness. For Nevin, the public tendency to regard any sense of the universal as a collectivity of individuals is a misrepresentation of the truth of Christ. The individual and the collectivity are both abstractions that fail to comprehend the concrete sociality in which all existence takes place, however fragmented it may be in our thinking. America is the theater, providing the stage, on which diversity is not permitted to absolutize its myriad claims to truth, but must be open to a wholeness that is greater than the sum of its parts. Nevin's idea of catholicity as wholeness offers fertile ground for the development of a theology that acknowledges the pluralism of the social and religious orders. It is a facet of his religious thought that awaits further investigation.

History is an elusive enterprise. It is the vision of the duration of human activity, a vision that leads to the telling of stories meant to provide for our identity, our sense of rootedness and ongoingness. History is the way we think of our being-in-the-world. Without a sense of history we would be lost in space. History is the arena of human existence and includes whatever perception we have of other beings and worlds. There is a cosmic and catholic dimension to our awareness of existence that demands the constant reworking of our history. At the time of the colonization of North America the European historical vision had closed in upon itself, forcing the growth of an eschatological hope that focused on a "land promised to the saints." At times the hope emphasized the end of history; at other times it was invested in the role of the promised land in the history of the redemption of the world. American religion began to develop as a message of salvation that was an escape from history. For many people it became a "blessed assurance" for the individual "soul" fixed, as Paul Boyer has shown, on the occasion "when time shall be no more."[2] For others religion became the spiritual resource for a successful life without the drag of history.

John Nevin's theology took full account of the importance of history. The idea of the Incarnation required history and provided an understanding of it. The new creation was a reality that gave internal significance and effective force to the external circumstances of human existence. Without that significance and vitality, for Nevin, there was no real history.

The understanding of radical catholicity, so prominent in Nevin's thinking, had implications for the understanding of the American Republic. For Nevin, America was a theater for the enactment of a new stage in history. It required a movement beyond nationalism, which he basically understood as individualism collectively considered. On the subject of missions, too, Nevin recognized the responsibility for helping the peoples of the world to acknowledge and interpret the presence of the new creation in the elements of society and culture. Here again, catholicity required a movement beyond individualistic salvationism into a vocational concern for the shaping of civilization. The Church lives in the world with a special voice. It carries the text of the mystical union between Christ and the world. Liturgy is a transcript of that union making possible its celebration and reenactment. As I have shown, Nevin's religious thought addresses the public world in which the Christian Church worships. The worship of American Churches is found wanting because it gives no evidence of the sacramental character of the mystical presence of Christ. It focuses instead on private experience, private judgment, and Biblicism. The radical catholicity of the Incarnation is sacramental and liturgical.

John Nevin's theology is a complete system even though it is not a systematic theology. His ideas deserve a more receptive reading from both scholars and religious seekers. He challenges the canon of American religious thought. And the heart of that challenge beats with concern for the community of faith, for the body that represents the presence of a new creation in the midst of the old. "On the American scene," writes Brian Gerrish, "it was Nevin who was the most eloquent advocate of the organic view of the Church. In this, and not only in his contributions to Calvin scholarship, lies his significance."[3]

Notes

1. John W. Nevin, *My Own Life: The Earlier Years* (Lancaster, Pa.: Historical Society of the Evangelical and Reformed Church, 1964), p. 2. These reminiscences originally appeared on a weekly basis in the *Reformed Church Messenger* during the early part of 1870.

2. Ibid., p. 20.

3. Frederick Gast, introduction to *The Life and Work of John Williamson Nevin, D.D., LL.D.* by Theodore Appel (Philadelphia: Reformed Church Publication House, 1889), p. v.

4. Sydney E. Ahlstrom, *A Religious History of the American People* (New Haven: Yale University Press, 1972), p. 620.

5. I prefer the designation Pennsylvania Dutch, inasmuch as that is what they call themselves. But scholars insist on the more pedantically correct label "German."

6. To this day many Pennsylvania Germans tend to refer to all white, English-speaking people as "die Englisch."

7. Appel, *Life and Work,* p. 98.

CHAPTER I

1. John W. Nevin, "Zacharius Ursinus," *Mercersburg Review* 3, no. 5 (Sept. 1851): 491.

2. This periodical changed its name several times throughout its history—indeed, even during Nevin's lifetime.

3. Philip Schaff, "What Is Church History," in Charles Yrigoyen, Jr., and George M. Bricker, eds., *Reformed and Catholic: Selected Historical and Theological Writings of Philip Schaff* (Pittsburgh: Pickwick Press, 1979), p. 25; Brian A. Gerrish, *Tradition and*

the Modern World: Reformed Theology in the Nineteenth Century (Chicago: University of Chicago Press, 1978), p. 57.

4. Philip Schaff, *What Is Church History?* (Philadelphia: J. B. Lippincott, 1846), p. 9.

5. John W. Nevin, *The Mystical Presence: A Vindication of the Reformed or Calvinistic Doctrine of the Holy Eucharist* (Philadelphia: J. B. Lippincott, 1846), pp. 3–4. From a facsimile reprint by Archon Books, Hamden, Connecticut, 1963; introduction ("The World of Mercersburg Theology") by Richard E. Wentz.

6. Ibid., p. 15.

7. See R. Laurence Moore, *Religious Outsiders and the Making of Americans* (New York: Oxford University Press, 1986), p. xi. The entire book is a development of this hypothesis.

8. Glenn R. Hewitt, *Regeneration and Morality: A Study of Charles Finney, Charles Hodge, John W. Nevin, and Horace Bushnell* (Brooklyn, N.Y.: Carlson Publishing, 1991), p. 93.

9. James Hastings Nichols, *Romanticism in American Theology: Nevin and Schaff at Mercersburg* (Chicago: University of Chicago Press, 1961).

10. Luther J. Binkley, *The Mercersburg Theology* (Lancaster, Pa.: Franklin and Marshall College, 1953), p. 7, emphasis added.

11. Ibid., p. 140.

12. Ibid., p. 9.

13. Claude Welch, *Protestant Thought in the Nineteenth Century. Vol. 1, 1799–1870* (New Haven: Yale University Press, 1972), esp. pp. 227–233; Sydney E. Ahlstrom, *Theology in America* (Indianapolis: Bobbs-Merrill, 1967), esp. chap. 8.

14. James Ward Smith and A. Leland Jamison, eds., *The Shaping of American Religion* (Princeton, N.J.: Princeton University Press, 1961). This is the first volume in the Religion in American Life series.

15. Theodore Appel, *The Life and Work of John Williamson Nevin* (Philadelphia: Reformed Church Publication House, 1889), p. 30.

16. Robert T. Handy, *A Christian America* (New York: Oxford University Press, 1971), esp. pp. 3–64.

17. See Timothy L. Smith, *Revivalism and Social Reform in Mid-Nineteenth-Century America* (Nashville, Tenn.: Abingdon Press, 1957); John R. Bodo, *The Protestant Clergy and Public Issues, 1812–1848* (Princeton N.J.: Princeton University Press, 1954); Nancy A. Hardesty, *Your Daughters Shall Prophesy* (Brooklyn, N.Y.: Carlson Publishing, 1991).

18. Nevin, *My Own Life,* pp. 18–19.

19. Ibid., p. 29.

20. Ibid., p. 36.

21. Ibid., p. 140.

22. Ibid., p. 89.

23. Ibid., p. 90.

24. Hewitt, *Regeneration and Morality,* p. 107.

25. Nevin, *My Own Life,* p. 110.

26. Ibid., p. 115.

27. Ibid.

28. See Nathan O. Hatch, *The Democratization of American Christianity* (New Haven: Yale University Press, 1989).

29. Richard Weiss, *The American Myth of Success* (Urbana: University of Illinois Press, 1988), p. 30.

30. Nevin, *My Own Life,* p. 139.

31. George W. Richards, *History of the Theological Seminary of the Reformed Church in the United States, 1825–1934, Evangelical and Reformed Church, 1934–1952* (Lancaster, Pa.: Theological Seminary of the Evangelical and Reformed Church, 1952), p. 273.

32. John W. Nevin, "Eulogy on Doctor Rauch," *Mercersburg Review* 11, no. 3 (July 1859): 463.

33. John W. Nevin, *The Anxious Bench,* in Charles Yrigoyen, Jr., and George H. Bricker, eds., *Catholic and Reformed: Selected Theological Writings of John Williamson Nevin* (Pittsburgh: Pickwick Press, 1978), pp. 21, 29, 98.

34. John W. Nevin, "Catholic Unity," in Appel, *Life and Work,* p. 220.

35. Ibid., p. 223.

36. Nevin, *Mystical Presence,* p. 6.

37. Ibid., p. 256.

38. John W. Nevin, *History and Genius of the Heidelberg Catechism* (Chambersburg, Pa.: Publication Office of the German Reformed Church, 1847), p. iv.

39. Ibid., p. 137.

40. John W. Nevin, *The Church* (Chambersburg, Pa.: Publication Office of the German Reformed Church, 1847), pp. 4–6, 14.

41. John W. Nevin, "The Sect System," *Mercersburg Review* 1, no. 5 (1849): 482–507; no. 6 (1849) 521–539.

42. John W. Nevin, *The Antichrist* (New York: Taylor, 1848).

43. Ibid., p. 92.

44. See Richard E. Wentz, "John Williamson Nevin and American Nationalism," *Journal of the American Academy of Religion* 58, no. 4 (1991): 617–632; John W. Nevin, "The Year 1848," *Mercersburg Review* 1, no. 1 (1849): 10–44.

45. Nevin, "The Year 1848," p. 30.

46. Will Herberg, *Protestant, Catholic, Jew* (Garden City, N.Y.: Doubleday, 1960), p. 265.

47. Nevin, *The Anxious Bench,* p. 99.

48. John W. Nevin, "Early Christianity," part 3, *Mercersburg Review* 4, no. 1 (Jan. 1852): 53–54.

49. John W. Nevin, "Brownson's Quarterly Review," *Mercersburg Review* 2, no. 1 (Jan. 1850): 33.

50. Letter from J. W. Nevin to J. A. McMaster, dated February 26, 1853. University of Notre Dame Archives.

51. John W. Nevin to J. A. McMaster, Mercersburg, Pa., February 26, 1853 (University of Notre Dame Archives, Notre Dame, Ind.).

52. John W. Nevin, "Lectures on History," in Appel, *Life and Work* p. 598.

53. Appel, *Life and Work,* p. 477.

54. Ibid., p. 480.

55. Ibid., pp. 634–654.

56. John W. Nevin, "Judgment and Duty," *German Reformed Messenger* 26, no. 21 (Jan. 16, 1861): 2.

57. John W. Nevin, "Education," *Mercersburg Review* 18 (Jan. 1871): 18.

58. Appel, *Life and Work,* p. 719.

59. Nichols, *Romanticism,* p. 203.

60. Appel, *Life and Work,* p. 767.

CHAPTER 2

1. Hatch, *Democratization of American Christianity,* p. 166.

2. Ibid., p. 183.

3. See Richard E. Wentz, "The Leveller and the Aristocrat: Some Thoughts on American Religion and Society" (The Rita and William H. Bell Lecture, University of Tulsa, Jan. 20, 1991).

4. Emanuel V. Gerhart, *Institutes of the Christian Religion,* 2 vols. (New York: A. C. Armstrong, 1891, 1894); Nichols, *Romanticism,* p. 140.

5. Klaus Penzel, ed., *Philip Schaff, Historian and Ambassador of the Universal Church* (Macon, Ga.: Mercer University Press, 1991), p. xxxviii; also Gerrish, *Tradition and the Modern World,* p. 51; Appel, *Life and Work,* p. 225.

6. Philip Schaff, *The Principle of Protestantism* (Chambersburg, Pa.: Publication Office of the German Reformed Church, 1845), pp. 154–168.

7. Binkley, *Mercersburg Theology,* p. 18.

8. John W. Nevin, "Early Christianity," part 2, *Mercersburg Review* 3, no. 6 (Nov. 1851): 521.

9. Nevin, *Mystical Presence,* pp. 20–21.

10. Michael Walzer, *The Revolution of the Saints* (Cambridge, Mass.: Harvard University Press, 1965), pp. 27–30.

11. John W. Nevin, "Catholicism," *Mercersberg Review* 3, no. 2 (1851): 12.

12. Ibid., p. 26.

13. Loren Eiseley, *The Man Who Saw Through Time* (New York: Charles Scribner's Sons, 1973), p. 99.

14. Quoted in ibid., p. 9.

15. Nevin, *Mystical Presence,* pp. 141–142.

16. Ibid., p. 142.

17. Ibid.

18. Ibid., p. 148.

19. Nevin, *The Anxious Bench,* p. 110.

20. Nevin, "Catholicism," p. 19.

21. John W. Nevin, *Human Freedom and a Plea for Philosophy: Two Essays* (Mercersburg, Pa.: P. A. Rice, "Journal Office," 1850), p. 41.

22. Nevin, *Heidelberg Cathechism,* p. 114.

23. Ibid., p. 117.

24. Ibid., p. 128.

25. Ibid., p. 129.

26. Nevin, *The Anxious Bench,* p. 118.

27. Ibid., pp. 108–109.

28. Ibid., p. 106.

29. Ibid., pp. 99, 107, 109; emphasis added.

30. Nevin, *Mystical Presence,* p. 171.

31. Ibid.

32. Hewitt, *Regeneration and Morality,* pp. 113–123.

33. Ibid., p. 113.

34. Nevin, *Mystical Presence,* p. 173.

35. Hewitt, *Regeneration and Morality,* p. 119; emphasis added.

36. Ibid., p. 121.

37. Appel, *Life and Work,* pp. 615–616.

38. Nevin, *The Anxious Bench,* pp. 106–108; emphasis added.

39. Nevin, *Mystical Presence,* p. 56.

40. Ibid., p. 63.

41. Nevin, "The Year 1848," pp. 10–44.

42. John W. Nevin, "The Nation's Second Birth," *German Reformed Messenger* 30, no. 49, (1865): 1.

43. Nevin, "The Year 1848," pp. 28–29.

44. Nevin, *Mystical Presence,* p. 184; emphasis added.

45. Ibid., p. 245.

46. Ibid., p. 170.

47. Orestes Brownson, in *Brownson's Quarterly Review* 4 (1847): 473.

48. Nevin, *Mystical Presence,* p. 18.

49. Victor Turner, *The Ritual Process: Structure and Anti-Structure* (Baltimore: Penguin, 1974), p. 114.

50. Nevin, *The Church,* pp. 8–9.

51. Frederick A. Gast, in Appel, *Life and Work,* p. vii.

52. John W. Nevin, "Our Relations to Germany," *Mercersburg Review* 14 (Oct. 1867): 631.

53. Appel, *Life and Work,* p. 734.

54. Ibid., p. 732.

55. Ibid., p. 747.

56. Ibid.

57. David W. Noble, *The Eternal Adam in the New World Garden* (New York: George Braziller, 1968), p. 4.

CHAPTER 3

1. Anon., "American Theology", *Mercersburg Review* 19 (Apr. 1872): 291–292.

2. John W. Nevin, "Undying Life in Christ," in Apple, *Life and Work,* p. 622.

3. Schaff, *Principle of Protestantism,* pp. 155–158.

4. John W. Nevin, "Natural and Supernatural," *Mercersburg Review* 11, no. 2 (Apr. 1859); 176–210; quote on p. 178.

5. Ibid., p. 179.

6. Ibid., p. 180.

7. John W. Nevin, "Judgment and Duty," *German Reformed Messenger* 26, no. 20 (Jan. 1861): 2.

8. Quoted in John Joseph Stoudt, *Pennsylvania Folk-Art: An Interpretation* (Allentown, Pa.: Schechter's, 1948), pp. 50–51.

9. Klaus Penzel, ed., *Philip Schaff: Historian and Ambassador of the Universal Church* (Macon, Ga.: Mercer University Press, 1991), p. 216.

10. Ibid., p. 217.

11. George Shriver, *Philip Schaff: Christian Scholar and Ecumenical Prophet* (Macon, Ga.: Mercer University Press, 1987), p. 41.

12. Ibid., pp. 86–88.

13. John W. Nevin, "Pseudo-Protestantism," *Weekly Messenger of the German Reformed Church,* Sept. 10, 1845, n.p.

14. Nevin, *The Antichrist,* pp. 81–90, 92.

15. Quoted in Edwin S. Gaustad, *A Documentary History of Religion in America to the Civil War* (Grand Rapids, Mich.: William B. Eerdmans, 1982), pp. 472, 475.

16. Nevin, "Brownson's Quarterly Review," p. 52.

17. Ibid., p. 57.

18. Ibid., pp. 71, 74.

19. Robert W. Bellah, "Religion and the Legitimation of the American Republic," in Robert N. Bellah and Phillip E. Hammond, eds., *Varieties of Civil Religion* (San Francisco: Harper and Row, 1980), p. 12.

20. Nevin, "Judgment and Duty," p. 2.

21. Bellah, "New Religious Consciousness and the Crisis in Modernity," in *Varieties of Civil Religion,* p. 170.

22. Walter Brueggemann, *The Prophetic Imagination* (Minneapolis, Minn.: MN: Fortress Press, 1989), pp. 67–68.

23. Nevin, *My Own Life,* p. 69.

24. Nevin, "Brownson's Quarterly Review," p. 53.

25. Ibid., p. 33.

26. Cf. Orestes Brownson, review of Bancroft's *History of the United States,* vol. 4, in *Brownson's Quarterly Review* 9 (Oct. 1852), esp. pp. 423, 428.

27. Nevin, "Brownson's Quarterly Review," p. 71.

28. Ibid., p. 67.

29. Ibid., p. 33.

30. Nevin, "Catholicism," p. 26.

31. Ibid., p. 13.

32. Nichols, *Romanticism,* p. 202.

33. Nevin, "Early Christianity" part 3, pp. 42, 43.

34. Nevin, "Catholicism," p. 14.

35. John W. Nevin, "The Church Year," *Mercersburg Review* 8 (1856): 456–461.

36. Nevin, "Catholicism," p. 14.

37. Nevin, "Early Christianity," part 3, p. 40.

38. Edmund S. Morgan, *Visible Saints: History of a Puritan Idea* (Ithaca, N.Y.: Cornell University Press, 1987), passim.

39. Patricia U. Bonomi, *Under the Cope of Heaven: Religion, Society, and Politics in Colonial America* (New York: Oxford University Press, 1988), p. 219.

40. Jon Butler, *Awash in a Sea of Faith* (Cambridge, Mass.: Harvard University Press, 1990), passim.

41. Bonomi, *Under the Cope of Heaven,* p. 217.

42. Cf. H. Richard Niebuhr, *Christ and Culture* (New York: Harper and Row, 1951), esp. chaps. 2 and 5.

43. Nancy A. Hardesty, *Your Daughters Shall Prophesy: Revivalism and Feminism in the Age of Finney* (Brooklyn, N.Y.: Carlson Publishing, 1991), p. 32.

44. Ibid., p. 13.

45. Mark C. Carnes, *Secret Ritual and Manhood in Victorian America* (New Haven: Yale University Press, 1989), p. 114.

46. Horace Bushnell, *Christian Nurture* (New York: Scribner, 1861), p. 237.

47. Carnes, *Secret Ritual,* p. 111.

48. Nevin, *Anxious Bench,* p. 95.

49. Nevin, *My Own Life,* p. 89.

50. Ibid., p. 93.

CHAPTER 4

1. Nevin, "Catholicism," pp. 5–6.

2. Nevin, "The Year 1848," p. 39.

3. Ibid.

4. John W. Nevin, "Bible Anthropology," *Mercersburg Review* 24 (July 1877): 359.

5. Ibid.

6. Ibid.

7. Ibid.

8. Nevin, "Brownson's Quarterly Review," p. 65.

9. John W. Nevin, "The Mystical Union," *Weekly Messenger,* Oct. 8, 1845, p. 2091.

10. Ibid.

11. Ibid.

12. Ibid.

13. Ibid.

14. Nevin, "Judgment and Duty."

15. Nevin, "The Mystical Union"; emphasis added.

16. Ibid.

17. Nevin, "Catholicism," p. 3.

18. Ibid., p. 7.

19. Ibid., p. 4.

20. Ibid., p. 11.

21. Ibid., p. 10.

22. Nevin, *Mystical Presence,* p. 245.

23. Nevin, "Catholicism," p. 17.

24. Ibid., p. 21.

25. Ibid.

26. T. S. Eliot, "East Coker," in *The Complete Poems and Plays, 1904–1950* (New York: Harcourt, Brace and World, 1971), pp. 123, 128.

27. Nevin, "Catholicism," p. 14.

28. Ibid., p. 17.

29. Nevin, "Early Christianity," part 3, p. 40.

30. Ibid., pp. 42–43.

31. Ibid., p. 43.

32. Ibid.

33. Nevin, "Catholicism," p. 6.

34. Ibid., p. 7.

35. John W. Nevin, "Christ and Him Crucified" (published by The Synod, Pittsburgh, 1863, p. 9).

36. Ibid., p. 11.

37. Ibid., p. 12.

38. Ibid., p. 16.

39. Nevin, "The Sect System," p. 507.

40. John W. Nevin, "Early Christianity," part 2, p. 538.

41. Hewitt, *Regeneration and Morality,* p. 105.

42. John W. Nevin, "Nature and Grace," *Mercersburg Review* 19 (Oct. 1872): 488. Nevin translated "born again" (as found in St. John's Gospel, 3: 1–7) as "born from above."

43. Nevin, "Catholicism," p. 26.

CHAPTER 5

1. Appel, *Life and Work,* p. 596.

2. Nevin, *My Own Life,* p. 139.

3. Gerrish, *Tradition and the Modern World,* p. 199, n. 19.

4. Nevin, *My Own Life,* p. 143.

5. Ibid.

6. Ibid.

7. Frederick Turner, *Beyond Geography: The Western Spirit Against the Wilderness* (New York: Viking Press, 1980), p. 35.

8. From Giles Gunn, *New World Metaphysics* (New York: Oxford University Press, 1981), pp. 138–139; emphasis added.

9. Ibid., pp. 173–174.

10. Ibid., p. 171.

11. Nevin, *Human Freedom* p. 31.

12. Nevin, *The Anxious Bench*, p. 29.

13. Nevin, *Mystical Presence*, p. 106.

14. Gerrish, *Tradition and the Modern World*, p. 60.

15. Nevin, *The Anxious Bench*, p. 43.

16. Ibid., p. 71.

17. Nevin, "The Sect System," p. 71.

18. Ibid., p. 485.

19. John W. Nevin, "The Philosophy of History" (Lectures recorded at Franklin and Marshall College, S. S. Kohler, class of 1875).

20. Nevin, "The Sect System," p. 485.

21. Ibid., pp. 486–487.

22. Ibid., p. 495.

23. Ibid., p. 495.

24. Ibid., p. 504.

25. Ibid., p. 499.

26. Nevin, "Early Christianity," *Mercersburg Review* 3 (Sept. 1851): 477.

27. Ibid., p. 480.

28. Ibid., p. 481.

29. Ibid.

30. Ibid., p. 483.

31. Ibid.

32. John W. Nevin, "The Anglican Crisis," *Mercersburg Review* 3 (July 1851): 359.

33. Ibid., p. 360.

34. Ibid., p. 361.

35. Ibid., p. 377.

36. Ibid., p. 378.

37. John W. Nevin, "The New Creation in Christ," Mercersburg Review 2 (Jan. 1850): 4.

38. Ibid., p. 7.

39. Nevin, "Catholicism," pp. 7–8.

40. Nevin, "New Creation," p. 7.

41. Ibid., p. 11.

42. Nichols, *Romanticism*, p. 137.

43. Schaff, *Principle of Protestantism*, pp. 220–221, 227.

44. Ibid., pp. 46–47.

45. Ibid., p. 43.

46. Nevin, "The Year 1848," pp. 17, 20–22, 39.

47. Nevin, "Philosophy of History" (Lecture III).

48. Nevin, "The Year 1848," pp. 30, 37.

49. Binkley, *Mercersburg Theology,* p. 30; Appel, *Life and Work,* p. 596.

50. Nichols, *Romanticism,* p. 115.

51. Nevin, "Philosophy of History" (Lecture XIV).

52. Nevin, *Human Freedom,* p. 5.

53. Ibid., p. 7.

54. Nevin, "Philosophy of History" (Lecture XIV); Appel, *Life and Work,* p. 597.

55. Appel, *Life and Work,* p. 597.

56. Ibid.

57. Pierre Teilhard de Chardin, *How I Believe* (New York: Harper and Row, 1969), p. 77.

CHAPTER 6

1. Nevin, "The Year 1848," pp. 28–30.

2. Ibid., pp. 30, 33.

3. Ibid., p. 32.

4. Ibid., p. 30.

5. Ibid., p. 31.

6. Ibid., pp. 31–32.

7. Ibid., p. 31.

8. Winthrop S. Hudson, *Nationalism and American Religion* (New York: Harper and Row, 1970), p. 56.

9. James D. Bratt, "Nevin's Life and Work in Political-Cultural Context," *New Mercersburg Review,* no. 2 (Autumn 1986): 21.

10. Appel, *Life and Work,* p. 119.

11. Ibid., p. 123.

12. Nevin, "The Year 1848," p. 29.

13. Ibid., p. 42.

14. Ibid.

15. Nevin, *Mystical Presence,* p. 201.

16. Robert N. Bellah, *The Broken Covenant* (New York: Seabury Press, 1975), p. 23.

17. See Orestes Brownson, *Brownson's Quarterly Review* 4, (1848): 473–474.

18. Bellah, *Broken Covenant,* p. 24.

19. Robert N. Bellah and Phillip E. Hammond, *Varieties of Civil Religion* (San Francisco: Harper and Row, 1980), pp. 169–170.

20. Ibid., p. 170.

21. Nevin, "The Sect System," p. 495.

22. Sidney E. Mead, *The Lively Experiment* (New York: Harper and Row, 1963), p. 135.

23. Nicolas Berdyaev, *The Destiny of Man* (London: Geoffrey Bles, 1948), p. 114.

24. Nevin, "Catholicism," p. 11.

25. Sacvan Bercovitch, "The Biblical Basis of the American Myth," in Giles Gunn, ed., *The Bible and American Arts and Letters* (Philadelphia: Fortress Press, 1983), p. 226.

26. Nevin, "Catholicism," p. 3.

27. Nevin, "The Year 1848," p. 33.

28. Ibid.

29. Ibid., p. 31.

30. Nevin, "Catholicism," p. 19.

31. Henry F. May, *Ideas, Faith and Feelings: Essays on American Intellectual and Religious History, 1952–1982* (New York: Oxford University Press, 1983), p. 53.

32. Ralph Ketcham, *Individualism and Public Life* (New York: Basil Blackwell, 1987), p. viii.

33. Nevin, *The Anxious Bench*, pp. 98–99.

34. Quoted in Gaustad, *A Documentary History of Religion*, p. 337.

35. Nichols, *Romanticism*, p. 3.

36. James I. Good, *History of the Reformed Church in the United States in the Nineteenth Century* (New York: 1911), p. 312.

37. John W. Nevin, "Educational Religion," *Weekly Messenger*, July 7, 1847, p. 2458.

38. Ibid.

39. Nevin, "Catholicism," p. 17.

40. Ibid., p. 10.

41. "The Nation's Second Birth," p. 1.

42. Ibid.

43. Ibid.

44. Ibid.

45. Ibid.

46. Ibid.

47. Ibid.

48. Nevin, "Catholicism," p. 33.

49. Nevin, "The Nation's Second Birth."

CHAPTER 7

1. Nevin, "Catholicism," p. 17.

2. Martin E. Marty, *Righteous Empire* (New York: Harper and Row, 1970), p. 54.

3. R. Pierce Beaver, "Missionary Motivation Through Three Centuries," in Jerald C. Brauer, ed., *Reinterpretation in American Church History* (Chicago: University of Chicago Press, 1968), p. 127.

4. Ibid., p. 113.

5. Jonathan Edwards, "Some Thoughts Concerning the Revival," in C. C. Goen, ed., *The Works of Jonathan Edwards: The Great Awakening* (New Haven: Yale University Press, 1972), p. 353.

6. Beaver, "Missionary Motivation," p. 126.

7. Ibid., p. 126.

8. John W. Nevin, "Religious Selections," *Weekly Messenger,* May 31, 1843, p. 1.

9. Ibid.

10. Nevin, "The Anxious Bench," p. 115.

11. "Religious Selections," p. 1.

12. Ibid.

13. Ibid.

14. Binkley, *Mercersburg Theology,* p. 87.

15. Gerrish, *Tradition and the Modern World,* p. 70.

16. John W. Nevin, "The Doctrine of the Reformed Church on the Lord's Supper," *Mercersburg Review* 2, no. 5 (Sept. 1850): 421–548.

17. Nevin, "The Church Year," pp. 456–461.

18. "Religious Selections," p. 1.

19. Ibid.

20. Nevin, "Catholicism," p. 17.

21. Linell E. Cady, *Religion, Theology, and American Public Life* (Albany: State University of New York Press, 1993), p. 26.

22. Ibid., p. 28.

23. Nevin, "Catholicism," p. 7.

24. Beaver, "Missionary Motivation," pp. 125–126.

25. Nevin, "The Sect System," p. 535.

26. Nevin, "Catholicism," p. 16.

27. Appel, *Life and Work,* p. 713ff.

28. Loren C. Eiseley, *The Star Thrower* (New York: Times Books, 1978), p. 296.

29. Henry Nash Smith, *Virgin Land* (Cambridge, Mass.: Harvard University Press, 1971), p. 37.

30. Quoted in ibid., p. 40.

31. Quoted in Appel, *Life and Work,* p. 458.

32. Nevin, "Judgment and Duty," p. 2.

33. Nevin, "Natural and Supernatural," p. 204.

34. Ibid., p. 210.

35. Handy, *A Christian America,* pp. 95–154.

36. John W. Nevin, "The Spirit of Prophecy," *Mercersburg Review* 24 (April 1877): 181.

37. Ibid.

38. Nevin, "Bible Anthropology," (July 1877): 364–365.

39. Nevin, "Catholicism," pp. 15–17.

40. John W. Nevin, "The Spiritual World," *Mercerburg Review* (October 1876): 504.

CHAPTER 8

1. John W. Nevin, "Theology of the New Liturgy," *Mercersburg Review* 14 (Jan. 1867): 27.

2. Richards, *History of the Theological Seminary,* p. 337.

3. Tom F. Driver, *The Magic of Ritual* (San Francisco: Harper and Row, 1991), p. 5.

4. Ibid., pp. 12–13.

5. Henry F. May, *Ideas, Faiths and Feelings* (New York: Oxford University Press, 1983), p. 118.

6. Ibid., p. 149.

7. Binkley, *Mercersburg Theology,* pp. 100, 116.

8. Jon Butler, *Awash in a Sea of Faith* (Cambridge, Mass.: Harvard University Press, 1990), see esp. chap. 2.

9. H. M. J. Klein, *History of the Eastern Synod of the Reformed Church in the United States* (Lancaster, Pa.: Eastern Synod, 1943), p. 6.

10. Charles H. Glatfelter, *Pastors and People: German Lutheran and Reformed Churches in the Pennsylvania Field, 1717–1793* (Breinigville, Pa.: Pennsylvania German Society, 1980), p. 3.

11. Richards, *History of the Theological Seminary,* pp. 332–337.

12. Binkley, *Mercersburg Theology,* p. 105.

13. John W. Nevin, *Vindication of the Revised Liturgy* (Philadelphia: Reformed Church Publication Society, 1867); "Theology of the New Liturgy," pp. 23–66.

14. John W. Nevin, "The Liturgical Movement," *Mercersburg Review* 1, no. 6 (Nov. 1849): 611.

15. Ibid., pp. 611–612.

16. Ibid., p. 612.

17. Nevin, *Mystical Presence,* p. 199.

18. Ibid., p. 215.

19. Ibid.

20. Nevin, "The Church Year," p. 462.

21. Ibid., p. 467.

22. Ibid.

23. Ibid., p. 469.

24. Ibid., p. 471.

25. Ibid.

26. Ibid., p. 472.

27. Ibid., p. 474.

28. Ibid., p. 477.

29. Ibid., p. 478; emphasis added.

30. Nevin, "Theology of the New Liturgy," p. 27.

31. Binkley, *Mercersburg Theology,* p. 102.

32. Nevin, *The Anxious Bench,* p. 47.

33. Nevin, "Theology of the New Liturgy," p. 28.

34. Nevin, "Catholicism," p. 19.

35. Ibid.

36. Nevin, "Theology of the New Liturgy," p. 30.

37. Ibid., p. 33.

38. Ibid.

39. Ibid., p. 34.

40. Ibid., p. 35.

41. Ibid., pp. 37–38.

42. Ibid., p. 40.

43. Ibid., p. 41.

44. Ibid., p. 42.

45. Ibid., p. 44.

46. Ibid.

47. Ibid., p. 44.

48. Ibid.

49. Ibid., p. 50.

50. Ibid., pp. 51–52.

51. Ibid., pp. 34–35.

52. Nevin, *Mystical Presence,* p. 247.

53. Gerrish, *Tradition and the Modern World,* p. 62.

54. Ibid., p. 57.

55. Nevin, *Mystical Presence,* p. 249.

56. Ibid., pp. 249–250.

57. Ibid., p. 235.

58. T. S. Eliot, *The Complete Poems and Plays, 1909–1950* (New York: NY: Harcourt, Brace and World, 1952), p. 107.

59. Quoted in John W. Nevin, "Answer to Professor Dorner," *Mercersburg Review* 15 (Oct. 1868): p. 538.

60. Ibid.

61. Ibid., pp. 568–569.

62. Ibid., p. 569.

63. Ibid., p. 614.

64. Ibid., p. 615.

65. Ibid.

66. Ibid.

67. Ibid., p. 622.

68. Ibid., p. 623.

69. Ibid., p. 633.

70. Ibid., pp. 643, 644, 646.

CONCLUSION

1. Cushing Strout, *Making American Tradition* (New Brunswick, N.J.: Rutgers University Press, 1990), p. 1.

2. Paul Boyer, *When Time Shall Be No More* (Cambridge, Mass. Howard University Press, 1992).

3. Gerrish, *Tradition and the Modern World,* p. 69.

INDEX